"In the evolving world in which we live, *How to Leave the Law* is a wise and invaluable guide to lawyers considering change at every level of their careers. How I wish I'd had this book when I was a young attorney trying to 'leave the law'!"

MARIE BENEDICT, *New York Times* Best-Selling Author

"The Experts in Alternative Legal Careers, Brown and Impellizzeri have outdone themselves once again! 'Big law' veterans and long-time authors on alternative legal careers Liz Brown and Amy Impellizzeri come together to deliver superb advice not only about forging a new career path, but how, when and whether to make the break from traditional law in the first place. Their own career journeys are great examples of how to re-deploy a law degree, but that's only the beginning of the conversation. Their combination of 'lived experience,' deep research, and skill in interviewing and recounting the career paths of lawyers whose careers took off in a new direction yields recommendations that could only come from the two definitive experts on the topic."

CAROL FISHMAN COHEN, CEO and Co-founder, iRelaunch

"If you are thinking about leaving the practice of law, this is the book that you need to read first. *How to Leave the Law* is a fascinating, thorough, fair, and informative guide that will take the reader through every step of the process. The authors draw from their own experiences and an extraordinary amount of research as the basis for their clear, step-by-step guidance. Having made my own journey from my career as a law firm partner, I can attest that the authors well understand the complexity of the process and the need for helpful sources of advice. They provide this in abundance."

LAUREN STILLER RIKLEEN, President, Rikleen Institute for Strategic Leadership and Author of *The Shield of Silence: How Power Perpetuates a Culture of Harassment and Bullying in the Workplace*

HOW TO
LEAVE
THE
LAW

HOW TO LEAVE THE LAW

LIZ BROWN & AMY IMPELLIZZERI

Wyatt-MacKenzie Publishing
DEADWOOD, OREGON

HOW TO LEAVE THE LAW

Liz Brown & Amy Impellizzeri

ISBN: 978-1-948018-86-9
Library of Congress Control Number on file.

Wyatt-MacKenzie Publishing
DEADWOOD, OREGON

Wyatt-MacKenzie Publishing, Inc.
www.WyattMacKenzie.com
Contact us: info@wyattmackenzie.com

DEDICATION

From Amy: To Paul, Luke & Grace ... You will always be my favorite chapter.

From Liz: To the memory of my parents, Benson and Celia Brown, who exemplified lives well lived and helped me find both meaning and adventure in my own life. They are still, and always, my role models.

TABLE OF CONTENTS

Introduction

WE GET IT.

We understand from personal experience both how thrilling and how devastating change can be. In the nearly ten years since our first books about lawyers' career transitions came out, we have both been through some pretty significant transitions ourselves. Amy has become a best-selling novelist and a widely acclaimed podcast host. She and her husband of over 20 years divorced and she's launched one child from the nest as she gets ready to launch two more in the coming years.. Liz finally got some job security as a tenured professor, but experienced the loss of both of her deeply loved parents. We aren't even going to talk about the pandemic (for now, at least).

Our goal in writing this book is to provide you with some support, some wisdom, and a strong sense of community to help you through whatever changes you may be considering in your career. Maybe that is a short vacation. Maybe that is a three month "sabbatical." Maybe it is a complete career change. No single solution is right for everyone. And you may not even leave the legal profession, in the end. Although the title of this book may suggest otherwise, we don't think that you necessarily have to leave the law in order to be happy or to find yourself. While both of us left big firm litigation roles, our paths have been very different from each other's. The right path is as unique as the person who is following it.

What we want you to hear is this: whether you have earned a J.D. or are still in law school, whether you are a seasoned advocate or a junior associate, you have *options.* Lots of options. In fact, you have many more options than most lawyers ever hear about, which is why we wrote this book. Over the last several years, we have been thrilled to see a greater recognition of the options open to those of us who went to law school. There is a greater recognition that law schools teach people a wide range of skills that add value to any kind of enterprise, including critical thinking, persuasive reasoning, and written and oral communication skills. More people than ever before appreciate that those of us who have worked as lawyers can do much more than win a case or negotiate a contract. The versatility of a law degree and legal training has never been more profound.

But the work of change remains in your hands. You start to make a difference in your own life when you consider what could be different. Yes, you may be able to persuade someone to give you your dream job outside of traditional law practice, but you have got to have the dream first. Small steps can lead to big changes, but only if you are willing to take the small steps first. We are here to help you take those steps, and we will be here to cheer you on every step of the way. And in return, we ask you to pay it forward by continuing to deliver the message to aspiring and existing lawyers. As we grow the community of outspoken transitioning lawyers, we help broaden the community of support for those who cannot put a name to their dissatisfaction, who cannot shake free from their current inertia. By collecting and, importantly, disseminating, the stories of those lawyers who have written successful second (and third!) chapters, we are—all of us—creating a more robust and healthy population of former lawyers *and* practicing lawyers. Not everyone is meant to leave the law, after all, but if you are among those with a simmering desire to leave, we are here to show you *how.*

CHAPTER 1
The Changing Legal Profession

"[T]his has been a walk on the wild side to say the least."[1]
— Kalyn Johnson Chandler, former Big Law attorney turned Founder
and Creative Director of Effie's Paper

IN THE NEARLY TEN YEARS since *Life After Law* and *Lawyer Interrupted* were published, the legal profession has changed dramatically. Some of these changes happened as a result of the Covid-19 pandemic, but many of them resulted from trends that were in place well before the pandemic. While it used to be relatively easy to predict how a lawyer's career could evolve from any given starting point, those predictions are becoming less reliable all the time. It is increasingly hard to plan out a legal career in any sector of the profession because of these disruptions. As a result, lawyers need more professional flexibility than ever before. In this chapter, we will explore how these shifts in the practice of law have altered the landscape for lawyers at every stage of their professional lives so that you can put your own career shift in context.

The legal profession now looks more diverse and more fragmented than ever before. While starting salaries have never been higher for the subset of lawyers who go directly to large private firms, there is an increasing recognition both in the legal field, and for aspiring lawyers, that Big Law is not and cannot be the standard career path for most law school graduates. There are also increasingly broad "legal deserts" in many parts of the country where the lack of legal services makes it hard to get access to justice, and where lawyers are needed.

In the first year of the pandemic, many law firms announced layoffs of lawyers at every level of seniority. These layoffs shook the legal profession as thousands of lawyers scrambled to find new positions and new ways to pay off their significant student debt. The layoffs were reminiscent of the strife that hit the legal world during the Great Recession of 2009.[2] But this time, it is not clear that a rebound in the field is a certainty. As the pandemic eased, even the most stable law firms did not hire back all of the lawyers they had let go. Some have argued that since Big Law's layoffs have actually resulted in increased profits, they are not likely to increase their pre-pandemic numbers anytime soon.[3] Indeed, as we learned in 2009 and 2010, the pandemic-related law firm layoffs continue to be a vivid reminder that law firm jobs are just not as stable as they were even 20 years ago.

1. Technological Shifts Made Remote Lawyering Easier

Perhaps the biggest recent change in the legal profession relates to the adoption of new technology. Zoom became a critical tool for lawyers, clerks and judges during the pandemic. Lawyers working from home out of necessity met with colleagues and clients by Zoom. Parties negotiated settlements by Zoom. Attorneys took and defended depositions by Zoom. Hearings at all levels, from parking violations to arguments before the Supreme Court, were held online, an anomaly most seasoned lawyers will admit they would never have predicted.

While lawyers were not unique in needing to move most of their work online, the impact of this technological shift was more profound for lawyers than for people in many other professions. The urgent adoption of online meeting platforms was particularly disruptive to the legal profession especially because lawyers are notoriously resistant to change. Law is a tradition-heavy practice that, in many instances, tends to view innovation with skepticism. The pandemic accelerated changes that might have taken years to adopt otherwise. The CIO at one law firm observed, "We've evolved 10 years in six weeks. I don't mean my firm, but the market. That's how dramatic of an effect it's had."[4] If lawyers had been given a choice, they probably would not have moved so much of the practice online so fast.

And of course, we had been given a choice: online meeting technology existed years before the pandemic. Many if not all of these changes could have happened much sooner. For the most part, on the eve of global shutdown in early 2020, lawyers were still choosing to fly across the country to meet with deponents. Litigators were still required to appear in person before any court in which they were arguing. It was the urgency of the pandemic and the removal of the in-person option, rather than a voluntary shift to cost-savings or practical solutions, that effected the shift online.

As it becomes safer to go back to practicing law in person, it is not clear that everyone will do so. The online experiments may have proved so successful that some elements of the practice of law will remain online. This is both because of efficiency and because working remotely makes life easier for many people, especially those who have significant caretaking responsibilities. Firms and clients appreciate how cost-effective meeting online is, and there is a real environmental benefit to reducing the travel associated with in-person meetings. There can also be a significant savings in real estate costs by adopting these changes long-term. Perkins Coie, for example, announced that its shift to a hybrid work model would result in a 24% contraction in its office footprint overall.

These shifts to hybrid law practice are also likely to stay with us because so many law firms have already invested in the technological infrastructure necessary to sustain them. The laptops and routers have been distributed; cybersecurity has been strengthened in order to mitigate the risk of data leaks. Why not continue to benefit from that investment? To the extent law firms have done business in person because tradition dictated it, rather than because working in person was more efficient or effective, those traditions are likely to die out. In law, as in so many other fields, the pandemic has revealed how many business practices have become sustained by habit more than by reason.

In one of the most unexpected side effects of the pandemic as it affected the practice of law, transitioning en masse to online practice also showed us that lawyers are, in fact, capable of more innovation in general than the legal profession has tended to adopt in the past. Although lawyers are generally more risk averse and resistant to change than many other professionals, we learned that the system doesn't break if we do things differently and take advantage of technological innovation. That may mean that law firms and courts become more open to transformative change in the future. The fact that so many changes have occurred in other areas of the legal profession in such a short period of time, as discussed below, may make those transformative changes effectively impossible to avoid.

2. Demographic Shifts Reveal Differences in Gender Parity and Stress

In August 2021, the American Bar Association released its Profile of the Legal Profession.[5] This annual survey collected data from over 4,000 members of the ABA and more detailed information from 1,500 senior lawyers. While the annual report has always included some surprising data, the 2021 Profile was especially important because it underscored how much the Covid-19 pandemic has changed the world of law practice for both law firms and individual lawyers.

One of the most interesting concepts to emerge from the 2021 ABA Profile is that the future of the legal profession is, increasingly, female. It is true that women still make up just over a third (38%) of the lawyers in the United States. But that percentage has risen in the last decade. In 2011, only 33% of United States lawyers were women. Gender diversity is outpacing racial and ethnic diversity, according to the ABA National Lawyer Population Survey. Lawyers of color made up 14.6% of the legal profession in 2021, just under three percentage points higher than the percentage of lawyers who were of color in 2011 (11.7%). And the percentage of Black lawyers in 2021 (4.7%) remains essentially the same as the percentage of Black lawyers in 2011 (4.8%).

While women make up a minority of current lawyers, the percentage of female law students is rising fast. There are more women in law school than men. This has been the case since 2016, when 50.3% of all students at ABA-accredited law schools in the United States were female. In 2020, the percentage of women students at those law schools rose to 54.1%. Women are entering law school in larger numbers every year, while the number of men in law school is continuing to decrease. According to the ABA, the number of male law students has declined every year for the past ten years, from 78,516 in 2010 to just 52,339 in 2020. The number of female law students has risen every year since 2016, going from 55,766 in 2016 to 61,949 in 2020. Women now make up more than 60% of the enrollees in 25 law schools. There are no law schools in which more than 60% of the enrollees are men.

What does this female future mean for the legal profession? If current gender dynamics are anything to go by, it portends an even more stressed-out group of lawyers. One downside of more virtual law practice is likely to be a blurring of the work/home divide. During the Covid-19 pandemic, the double burden of work and home was harder for female lawyers to bear than for male lawyers in general. More female lawyers (63%) than male lawyers (44%) said it was hard to keep work and home separate during the pandemic. More women (57%) than men (41%) reported that their work had been disrupted by family and home obligations. In addition, women were almost three times more likely to take on additional child care responsibilities during the pandemic than men (14% of female lawyers compared with 5% of male lawyers). One potential explanation for the gender disparity is that the percentage of female lawyers (42%) who live with dependent children is greater than the percentage of male lawyers (30%) who do. Another explanation is that women still bear the presumptive responsibility for child care in the United States regardless of their professional status, an issue we discuss in more detail in the next chapter.

But work/family balance is not the sole source of stress for women in the legal profession. In general, during the pandemic, a much greater percentage of women (60%) said that they felt overwhelmed by all the things they had to do than men (38%). And far more female lawyers (52%) than male lawyers (34%) reported experiencing stress about work due to factors such as gender imbalance in the workplace, lack of mentorship, sexual harassment, and other issues. Will this mean that more women leave the practice of law, even as a greater percentage of women are entering the profession? If more of the lawyers in the United States are female, and more female lawyers experience stress than male lawyers do, it stands to reason that the profession will need to change from the inside. But that assumption depends in part on the extent to which those women lawyers are promoted to levels of leadership that empower them.

Whether the increasing numbers of women entering the legal profession will change the culture of law firms in the coming decades is yet to be seen. Women continue to be underrepresented in law firm management. According to the 2020 ABA Model Diversity Survey, men filled 77% of law firm leadership positions, which included hiring partners, leaders of firmwide compensation committees, and highest governance committees. White women were in 20% of those leadership positions while only 3% of law firm leadership positions went to women of color.

Because the leadership of law firms tends to be even more male dominated than the general population of lawyers, it is reasonable to expect that gender balance at the highest levels of law firms will be very slow to evolve even as more women enter the profession. Unless law firms address the reasons for this imbalance in leadership, female lawyers will be underrepresented by the leaders who set workplace policies, evaluate contributions for compensation purposes, and generally create the culture of these firms.

For now, the prospects for women lawyers aspiring to firm

leadership do not look good. The ABA's 2020 data showed that male lawyers also had a significant edge over female lawyers in terms of promotion. Male associates were more likely to be promoted to equity partnerships, while female associates were more likely to be promoted to non-equity partnerships. But attrition also plays a role in changing the profile of top-level lawyers. Female lawyers are more likely to leave law firms than male lawyers, according to the same study, and lawyers of color are twice as likely to leave a law firm as white lawyers.

3. Alternative Legal Services Diversify Legal Practice

Clients are no longer as dependent on lawyers in law firms as they used to be. The rise of self-help legal sites like LegalZoom, Nolo, and Boundless has made it easier and less risky to deal with many small stakes legal issues than it used to be. From an institutional perspective however, the more significant shift over the past decade is the expansive growth of alternative legal service providers, or ALSPs. ALSPs give corporate and individual clients another option in addition to traditional law firms, which can be especially valuable for discrete and limited tasks. ALSPs are attractive alternatives to law firms because they tend to be less expensive, more responsive, and more agile than the traditional firm structure.

Many ALSPs specialize in a particular niche, so they can offer specific expertise at a lower cost than most firms. ALSPs are most often used for electronic discovery, legal research and support for litigation, and pre-litigation investigations. Companies who do not want to pay for the overhead of law firms often prefer to use ALSPs for smaller projects like contract management. Increasingly, law firms themselves also turn to ALSPs to outsource tasks that were once done in-house, such as legal research and document review. According to one study, nearly 80 percent of law firms and more than 70 percent of corporate law departments now use ALSPs.[6] The ALSP market grew to almost $14 billion by the end of 2019, according to a 2021 report.

As attractive as ALSPs are to clients and firms, they can be even more attractive to lawyers who are looking for a new way to practice. The pyramid structure of law firms does not allow for everyone who starts as an associate to progress up to the partner level. More importantly, many lawyers find the billable hour requirements and bureaucracy of traditional law firm management too stressful and incompatible with their own personal and professional goals. ALSPs offer another way to practice law and an appealing alternative to law firms in general.

Some ALSPs specialize in offering more flexible work options to their attorneys. Axiom is one of the largest ALSPs to promote this model, and provides a good illustration of their appeal. Lawyers who work for Axiom have the flexibility to choose when they work and which projects to take on. They can choose to take long breaks between assignments. Because Axiom's basic model relies on remote work, it is especially easy to work from anywhere. Axiom hires from bases in cities all over North America and Europe. One of the tradeoffs with a model like Axiom's is that there is comparatively little training on the job. Axiom's job openings require a greater degree of specialization and a demonstrated ability to self-manage than law firms generally do. Clients get more flexibility when working with a company like Axiom than they would with a traditional law firm, in that they can hire lawyers for specific projects or hire lawyers on secondment for longer-term internal engagements.

ALSPs represent the kind of adaptive innovation to changes in the legal services market that have emerged in other fields as well. As David Wilkins and Maria Jose Esteban Ferrer point out in their article, "Taking the Alternative Out of Alternative Legal Service Providers," calling these providers "alternative" tends to undermine both the importance of these adaptive models and to mask the fact that the old, or original, models of law firms are likely to become less common in the coming decades.[7] We agree.

As Wilkins and Ferrer note, the evolution of ALSPs signals a larger shift. They predict that "the ecosystem in which both law firms and a wide range of other providers will compete is one that will increasingly require the integration of law into broader "business solutions" that allow sophisticated corporate clients to develop customized, agile, and empirically verifiable ways of solving complex problems efficiently and effectively." After talking with lawyers both inside the field and those transitioning from the traditional practice of law, we can't help but agree with Wilkins and Ferrer that these developments will continue to change what it means to be a lawyer and how law firms should offer services, as well as raise "critical questions about how to preserve traditional ideals of predictability, fairness, and transparency at the heart of what we mean by the rule of law." The rise of ALSPs, then, is only one part of a fundamental and ongoing shift in the legal profession.

4. Lawyers Think Differently About Career Trajectories

One major shift in the workforce that resulted from the pandemic is what some writers have called "The Great Resignation." This term refers to the massive shift in the labor force that took place in 2021, in which an unprecedented number of people are reconsidering the meaning and value of their work lives. Indeed, it's been difficult to pin down precise numbers of how many lawyers were laid off or voluntarily resigned as a result of, or during the pandemic.

Unmoored from their work routines by the pandemic, millions of people are stepping back to think differently about how they spend their time at work as well as what they do with their non-working time. In April 2021 alone, four million people quit their jobs. When large numbers of people quit their jobs, it is often a sign that the economy is healthy and people feel financially secure. But that was not the case in the pandemic, which led to the worst recession in U.S. history. While employers across the country complained of labor shortages, millions of people remained out of work. Many observers concluded that this was because people, in general, wanted more of the flexibility that the pandemic gave them in terms of where and how they could work. Increased personal losses, the illnesses and deaths of loved ones, and mental health issues caused by and exacerbated by Covid-19 may also have changed how people look at the time they spend at work and at home.

The Covid-19 pandemic also changed the way many lawyers think about their professional future, especially those who are closer to retirement age. The pandemic affected the way one-third of all "older" lawyers, defined as lawyers who are 62 and older, thought about retirement, according to the 2021 ABA Profile. These older lawyers did not all reach the same conclusion about changes to their retirement plans, however. Just over half of the senior lawyers who said that the pandemic had changed their plans indicated that they were going to delay their retirement. Just under half of these lawyers decided to do the opposite, and retire sooner than they had originally planned.

According to the ABA, this split in retirement plan impact may have had something to do with the fact that the pandemic did not have the same effect on income for all senior lawyers. More than a third of older lawyers (36%) reported making less money than they had before the pandemic. Nearly half of senior lawyers said that their income was more or less the same as it had been before.

But the reasons senior lawyers gave for changing their retirement plans vary widely. For those who decided to retire sooner than they had originally planned, the pandemic was a kind of wake-up call, reminding them that their time is too precious to waste on an unsatisfying career. One lawyer noted that the pandemic "made me realize that life is short, perhaps I should pull the plug while I can." Another responded that "the pandemic forced me to think about whether I wanted to do this anymore. Answer: NO."

For senior lawyers who decided to delay retirement in the wake of the pandemic, the increased flexibility of working from home appeared to play a big role. One noted that the pandemic "enabled me to work remotely from Florida and made the retirement transition easier." According to another, "Because it became more apparent that I could work remotely, I think it has made me more likely to just slow down a bit rather than retire." For these lawyers, it wasn't so much that the pandemic made them newly appreciative of how much they enjoyed the practice of law. It appeared to be more often the case that having more latitude in how and where they work made their careers easier to bear.

5. Law Schools Support More Diverse Professional Paths

These changes in the provision of legal services may be one factor in another trend we see. More law schools are acknowledging that their students won't follow one of the traditional career paths that most lawyers felt obligated to follow 10 or 20 years ago. When we graduated from law school, there was a general assumption that young lawyers would follow one of these paths (which we have grossly oversimplified for purposes of illustration):

1. Clerk and then go straight into public or private practice;
2. Private practice: start as an associate at a law firm and either (a) move up to the counsel or partner level or (b) move in-house after a few years of associate experience; or
3. Public service: start working for a government entity or a nonprofit and either (a) become more senior in that division of government, (b) lead a nonprofit, or (c) go into politics.

If you didn't choose one of those career paths, you would have been considered at least slightly deviant ten years ago. In 2013, few law students were exposed to alternatives to those traditional paths while they were still in school. The underlying assumption of the professional training that law schools offered was that the graduates would go on to practice law in one form or another. Unlike business schools, whose graduate programs envision a wide range of professional choices their graduates might make, law schools tended to cabin the future career paths of JDs more narrowly. Lawyers might choose different areas of law in which to specialize, and different law firm structures or public service roles, but those ways of differentiating oneself tended to crop up only after a law student had chosen one of those traditional paths.

Those traditional career paths still exist, of course, but are now just a few of the many different options that law schools prepare students to follow. In the past several years, some law schools have started to provide more accurate information to students about the wider range of non-traditional career paths available to them during their graduate education, rather than forcing them to figure it out on their own after they leave law school.

Berkeley Law, for example, offers support on its website to students and alumni considering non-legal careers. One of these resources is a nine-page list of "non-traditional jobs for law-trained professionals," with specific options in ten different fields including institutional advancement, corporate management, education, financial services, and the arts and media.[8] For each of these options, Berkeley Law suggests the key skills needed for each job as well as the background that will be most helpful for getting those jobs. Berkeley Law also offers a series of video and audio resources about non-traditional career paths for law school graduates. These include panel interviews with graduates who are working as management consultants as well as law school graduates who work in non-law jobs for law firms, including professional development and recruiting. Finally, Berkeley Law directs its students to several books in its Career Development Office library that support students who want to do something other than practice law after graduating from law school.

Other law schools have started introducing students to non-traditional career paths through innovative curriculum offerings and programs challenging the status quo. To that end, we applaud Professor Renee Knake Jefferson who, during her time at Michigan State, co-founded and secured substantial funding for the law school's inaugural program on technology, entrepreneurship, and innovation in legal services.[9] Other law schools whose creative and pioneering programs have caught our attention include Vanderbilt's Program on Law and Innovation, Stanford Law's Legal

Design Lab, and the Law and Innovation Lab at Sturm College of Law, just to name a few.

The impact of this kind of institutional support can't be over-stated. It is a lonely feeling to realize while you are still in law school that you don't actually want to follow a traditional career path. In the past, law schools offered little support or even recognition of this kind of professional dissonance. The acknowledgment and resources that law schools are now offering should mean that fewer law students feel forced into careers that are likely to make them miserable. This is especially true given the pull of debt that compels many law students to look for positions at large law firms, where starting salaries in some cities can exceed $200,000. The increase in average student loan debt over the past 20 years for people who finished law school is stunning. Between 2000 and 2016, that debt increased 77 percent, rising from $82,400 to $145,500.[10] Knowing that there are other financially viable ways of addressing that debt is more important now than it has ever been.

Some law schools also offer more support to alumni consider-ing alternative careers than they did 10 or 20 years ago, but these tend to be narrower in focus. For example, Harvard Law School tells its alumni that "one of the best things about a legal career is that it is extremely versatile and offers a wide range of profes-sional opportunities." There is a dedicated set of resources for alumni considering "alternative careers." With regard to "Career Transitions," however, Harvard Law School's website for alumni takes a narrower view of what those transitions might be to or from. Its advice on "Handling Career Change" offers advice in several specific scenarios, including "changing practice areas," "moving from a large firm to a small or medium firm," "re-entering the law after taking a leave" and, separately, "re-entering the law after staying home with kids." Notably, the alumni career services website does not offer structured advice for any transitions that do not involve either changing how one practices law or going back into law after some kind of break.

Of course, law school rankings continue to be based in part

upon the number of graduates they place in JD required positions[11], hampering many schools from truly encouraging their graduates to think outside the box. We continue to advocate for this criterion to be amended, and until it does, law school will continue to be as Amy has affectionately called it, the last legal pyramid scheme: with a primary mission to populate the bottom rungs of big law firms which seem to be constantly in need of new bodies as promotion and other factors (including stress and burnout and general attrition) empty out the various rungs of the law firm ladder.

Frustratingly, many local bar associations still focus their committees for "transitioning" lawyers on retiring lawyers, rather than lawyers who are making mid-career transitions. But this, too, is changing. We are gratified to report that law schools are not the only institutions now offering more support for JDs looking for non-traditional careers. In fact, the American Bar Association has also become somewhat more open to the idea that its members can pursue a wider range of options than it once envisioned, a trend that was first evidenced by its willingness to publish *Lawyer Interrupted* in 2015, a celebration of the versatility of the JD. These days, ABA's student-focused blog offers support for people who are still in law school and considering alternative paths. It underscores the fact that law school training prepares people for more than being an attorney. In the words of Ambrosio Rodriguez, a blogger for ABA For Law Students, "Law school changes the way you think and equips you with highly specialized analytical skills. Your new take on the world and the way you process information can help you in a number of different fields."[12] The ABA also offers support for lawyers who want to "leverage and pivot" later in their careers. Several articles on the "Alternative Careers" part of its website outline how lawyers can use their skills, training, and experience to succeed in several other non-legal careers. Additionally, the ABA provides some guidance on how to choose and pursue alternative careers as well as how to identify non-legal career options that are the best fit for you.[13]

The National Association for Law Placement (NALP) has also

accepted the idea that lawyers can and should consider alternatives to the traditional paths for lawyers, and now recognizes the importance of non-law placement as well. NALP offers a range of "alternative career handouts" on its website.[14] One of the most useful resources here is the "Before and After Resume," which illustrates how a lawyer can reshape her CV to qualify for a non-legal position; in this case, as the director of an alternative dispute resolution center. Building on alternative resume examples from Deborah Arron's *What Can You Do With a Law Degree?*, it shows how and why a lawyer can create a targeted resume that translates her professional experience into terms and a format that is easier for a non-legal employer to appreciate. More importantly, it shows how a lawyer can match her existing experience more closely to the specific requirements of a particular job listing, maximizing the chances that the employer will recognize the overlap between the candidate's skills and the required expertise. Not all of the NALP materials, however, are as supportive as they might be. NALP's advice on "services available to attorneys in transition" appears not to have been updated since 2006, and primarily helps lawyers learn what to look for in a career coach (something we will talk about in more detail and with more current information in Chapter 13).

Perhaps the best thing to have happened in the last ten years is the explosion of online and in-person resources for lawyers who want to make some kind of a professional change, and who are not sure how to do so. Many services have emerged to help support lawyers who want to know what they can do other than practice law. We list many of these in the directory in Appendix A, focusing on coaching services founded by and/or run by former lawyers. Why? Because lawyers have a unique educational experience and a common range of skills and preferences. For many years, lawyers who wanted to leave law had to work with general career coaches who could sympathize but not empathize with the kind of professional dissonance they were feeling. There were few career coaches who specialized in supporting lawyers in transition. Now, there are lawyer-specific resources in a broad range of media, including podcasts, videos, coaching programs in which groups of soon-to-be ex-lawyers work together with a coach, as well as one-on-one coaching options that we will discuss in more detail in Chapter 13.

This is a time of enormous disruption for lawyers. The world of law has changed dramatically over the past ten years, causing shifts in both the legal profession and in the resources available to those who want to leave. Some of these changes have resulted from technological innovations, allowing more people to work from home. Other changes were spurred specifically by the Covid-19 pandemic. Lawyers can do more things remotely than ever before because the judicial system and law firms have had to move critical functions online, in order to avoid grinding to a halt. The pandemic also changed the way many people, including but not limited to lawyers, felt about their careers and how they want to spend the rest of their working lives. The professional landscape has never been more varied. The resources available to JDs who want to leave the law have never been so wide-ranging. But how to find them? And how to sift through them judiciously and productively? That's what this book is meant to help you do.

The best way to start is to take a new look at the options that are available to you. Are you truly doing the work you love? Could you consider some small or large shifts in how you work, or what you do, that would bring you closer to that point? Can you take advantage of the disruptions in the legal profession and perhaps in your own world to make yourself more fulfilled at work and at home? In the pages that follow, we are going to show you how to identify and make the changes that you need in order to find a better working life.

Welcome to your next chapter!

CHAPTER 2

Challenges and Strategies for Caregivers

"Motherhood is demanding. [Lawyer moms are] exhausted."[15]
—Susan Smith Blakely

Cease and Desist or Fair Use?

IN STONE HARBOR, New Jersey, Springer's is a small but wickedly popular family-owned ice cream shop on Third Avenue just a few blocks from the beach. There's nowhere to eat inside the shop. It's a take-out only and cash only operation, and on any given summer night the line of customers winds down the block and around the corner, as Springer's shows off as one of the most visited spots in the beach town. There are 50+ flavors, but seasoned patrons know their favorites, and newbies figure out fast that they need to pick quickly, since the employees move even faster to accommodate the unending line each night. There's some attrition on the menu as the summer progresses, depending on the supply chain, but one flavor that generally stays well-stocked is a cult favorite: Cease & Desist.

Ask about the name, and you'll be pointed to the wall where a framed piece of mail on official letterhead resides. The letter references legal action Hershey and Company and its lawyers (who apparently fell asleep during the fair use lecture in their trademark classes) initiated against Springers, demanding they stop using the name of familiar Hershey candies on their menu board to describe flavors that included those candies. Springer's responded with the "Cease & Desist" flavor, a move which Hershey and its lawyers called "humorous" as they called off the legal action, thereby creating a funny story as you wait in line for ice cream at the beach. And also, we can't help but think, creating a perfect metaphor for parenting as a lawyer.

Day in and day out, lawyer caregivers are pretty much asked to do the incredible feat of renaming and reframing their identity for reasons not quite understandable, certainly not quite legal. Amy recalls her supervising partner telling her annually at her Skadden review: "Everyone loves you. Everyone gives you high praise. Everyone says they'd never even know you're a mom. Keep up the good work."

While the title of this book is also its message, we do find that far too many lawyer caregivers—especially parents—find themselves looking for a way out of the law prematurely. In fact, the only demographic of transitioning lawyers that consistently reports being dissatisfied with their transitions are those who leave the law prematurely to become full-time caregivers. Too many of us lawyer caregivers, and yes, a disproportionate amount of us are lawyer moms, find ourselves giving in to the cease and desist demands from our employers, but when are we going to argue for fair use instead?

Are We Fighting Fair?

In spite of Justice Ruth Bader Ginsburg's view that there will be enough women on the Supreme Court "when there are nine," women, who are over half of all law school applicants and half of all law school graduates, continue to make up a minority on the Supreme Court. Two of those women are unmarried and childless. The presence of Sonia Sotomayor and Elena Kagan, both nominated by President Barack Obama during his tenure in the White House, raises the necessary questions about the choices women today must make in order to achieve heights in their chosen careers, particularly in the legal field.

Indeed, few American lawyers, answering honestly, would cite coincidence that both Sonia Sotomayor and Elena Kagan are childless and highly successful lawyers. Most call Kagan and Sotomayor's paths ones of personal choice. No doubt. But framing the relevant issue as one of choice between children and career leaves American moms feeling marginalized. American lawyer moms feel even more so.

The issue is whether women in law have meaningful choices at all, beyond "motherhood versus success." Take for example, Barbara[16], a 50-year-old former Wall Street law firm partner. Barbara worked grueling hours and was awarded partnership at the age of 35 while still intentionally childless. Barbara then took an extended leave of absence while raising her two young children, relating that her decision to put off starting a family until after she made partner was a conscious one. "You just cannot do both," Barbara says emphatically. Polly, another former law partner in her 50s, describes a similar decision to put off starting a family until she was made partner, a trade-off she doesn't recall a single male in her firm having to make.

In a 2019 Report released by the ABA, Walking Out the Door[17], 45% of the women surveyed reported that they felt they'd been denied business development opportunities because of gender; this was in contrast to 6% of men who reported feeling the same way. And 67% of women lawyers reported a perception that they are less committed to the profession when they disclose their motherhood status.

The choice, at least in the legal field, is still framed in absolutes. High billables or personal life. Family or partnership. Motherhood or success.

Justice Ruth Bader Ginsburg would have rejected that binary framework, we think. And so would Justice Sandra Day O'Connor. Achieving the holy grail of a legal career, Justice O'Connor was appointed as the first female Supreme Court Justice back in 1981. Justice O'Connor's impressive resume included positions in private practice, in the Arizona state senate, and on the state appeals court. She was also a mother of three. Justice O'Connor did leave the law, albeit temporarily, for five years to raise her young children from 1960-1965. A choice? Sure. A choice between career and children? Not at all. Justice O'Connor took a short hiatus from private practice after the birth of her second son and subsequently relaunched her legal career in 1965 by joining the Arizona Attorney General's office.

And while not everyone can successfully navigate an impressive career with ebbs and flows that correspond with family responsibilities and demands, there are enormous numbers of women lawyers who do. Renee, a 43-year-old mother of two who worked as a Wall Street litigator for nine years and is now Assistant VP of a major insurance company, thinks there are still Sandra Day O'Connors out there. "The kids, viewed as a potential roadblock to a career for some, are actually a reflection of a person who can do it all, who can persevere in any environment, and thrive under any circumstances."

In her own professional journey, Renee thinks of the bumps and distractions as necessary and real as stretch marks. "Anyone can have a perfect stomach if they have never been pregnant ... and anyone can be a flawless professional if they do not have a tiny person waiting for them at home with perpetual, overwhelming, emotionally and physically all-consuming demands."

Gwen, a 54-year-old managing attorney with an international litigation support company, believes there are meaningful avenues of success for lawyer moms. But she does not believe for a minute that the sky is the limit. After spending over 12 years as a full-time Manhattan litigator and mom, Gwen became frustrated by what she perceived as a not-so-subtle ceiling for female litigators, particularly moms, and left for an eventual in-house directorship position with more power—and more flexibility. Gwen says that in her experience, outside the large law firm arena, there are more choices for today's female lawyers than just success or motherhood. However, Gwen cautions, "If you really seek greatness, e.g., the Supreme Court, not so much."

In her 2010 New York Times essay, "Judging Women," Lisa Belkin argued that the generational differences between Kagan and O'Connor are relevant. Belkin noted that for contemporaries of O'Connor and Ginsburg, for example: "Not much was given to or expected of women then, which created a paradoxical freedom."

Conversely for Sotomayor and Kagan's generation of female lawyers: "There would be no taking five years off to stay home with your children if you hoped for a seat on the Supreme Court." Ten years later, the confirmation of Amy Coney Barrett seemed to reinforce Belkin's argument, as Barrett, mother of seven, had no demonstrable gap in her resume, moving from clerkship to private practice to academia to the Court. And of course in 2022, the confirmation of Kentanji Jackson Brown was welcome and long overdue, but occurred after a public apology by Brown at her confirmation hearings in which she told her daughters: "Girls, I know it has not been easy as I have tried to navigate the challenges of juggling my career and motherhood. And I fully admit that I did not always get the balance right."

It's clear that the pressure that today's female lawyers feel to be present in their children's lives while still serving as examples to an entire generation can be daunting. Jessica Medina graduated from Columbia Law School as a single Latina mother of twins, and chose Big Law, motivated by hopes of creating both opportunity and comfort for her young family. When she decided not to put her name in for partner eight years later, she says she struggled. She recalls feeling like she was making a choice between her family and the Latina community who are traditionally underrepresented in Big Law partnership. Medina reconciled the choice by eventually starting her own company and currently is a financial consultant for would-be transitioning lawyers.[18]

But we've also talked to a generation of lawyers who continue to take hiatuses from huge billables and grueling work schedules to raise their young children before returning with vigor to rewarding and successful careers. Carol Fishman Cohen, co-founder of iRelaunch, has made it a personal mission to bring recognition to success stories of women in all fields, including the legal field, who relaunch their careers after multi-year breaks. Cohen lauds the renewed careers of lawyer moms like Deborah Felton, who relaunched her career as Executive Director of a Massachusetts senior community center after a twenty-year career break, and

Sara Harnish, who relaunched after a career break as Assistant Director of Non-Clinical Research at the Dana-Farber Cancer Institute before being named the Executive Chair of Advarra, a pharmaceutical research firm.

Of course, it would be helpful to give those hiatuses the same publicity we give the choices made by successful women like Kagan and Sotomayor. In fact, some high-profile successful relaunching lawyer moms have tried hard to keep their hiatuses under wraps. Lawyer mom Hillary Clinton campaigned for the job of first woman President on "35 years of experience," boasting that she worked as the first ever female partner at the Rose Law Firm from 1977 until 1993 when her husband won the presidency.

But even she did not work both jobs simultaneously the whole time. Strategic leaves of absence taken during the times when daughter, Chelsea, was a preschooler have been carefully described to avoid any appearance of resume gaps. During one eight-month leave from law firm life, when Chelsea was two, Clinton worked on her husband's gubernatorial campaign. And in 1983, when Chelsea was three, Hillary temporarily left her desk at the Rose Law Firm, agreeing to Chair the Arkansas Education Standards Committee. Clinton reportedly billed (and consequently earned) less than other partners during her tenure at the Rose Law Firm, and yet Clinton didn't campaign on a platform of work-life balance or part-time parity for lawyer moms.

How do we shift to a more humane model in the legal field in which we can stop demanding that parents, and specifically mothers, must cease and desist? We think the only way to demand more for lawyer moms and lawyer caregivers in general is to stop pretending and hiding and demanding trade-offs. In fact, we think that lawyer moms might not always need to leave the law after all.

But staying doesn't just mean that you should grin and bear it. Staying means taking a hard look at the systemic problems and working to change them from the inside out. Staying means agreeing to shine a spotlight on challenges rather than ignoring or dismissing them.

The Blakely Problem

In June 2021, Susan Smith Blakely, former law partner and current award-winning author of the *Best Friends at the Bar* series for female lawyers, caused a stir with an article published in the ABA Journal, entitled "Are Women Lawyers Paying Enough Attention to Upward Mobility?" Blakely cautioned women lawyers to be strategic and not get sidetracked. She cited pitfalls for the climb to success, apparently including having children:

"There are pitfalls. What works for women lawyers in the early years of practice may not work as well for them throughout their careers. And that is particularly true for women who choose to have children. There is nothing that can derail a career faster than the responsibilities of motherhood—ask any successful woman lawyer with children. It is a game changer that can cause very busy women lawyers to lose focus."[19]

While many have shuddered at her observations and verbiage, Blakely talks bluntly about the inordinate demands on lawyer moms' time, even when there's a parenting partner in the house. "Although many lawyer moms may have spouses and mates who help ease their burden at home, little children typically look to Mommy for on-time meals, rides to school before the morning bell rings, checking homework, and general comfort and care. And that is especially true when Daddy is a busy professional, too."[20]

And what about a post-COVID world? Well, Blakely acknowledges that just as COVID disrupted everyone's lives, it certainly disrupted those of lawyer moms. But, Blakely insists that post-COVID office models will not allow exceptions or accommodations for lawyer moms: "And the lawyer moms will be expected to meet the challenge just like everyone else."[21]

The reactions to Blakely's piece were swift and furious. Within a week, the ABA President, Patricia Lee Refo, published her own response (signed by 10 female ABA Presidents from the last 25 years) as the ABA tried to distance itself from the Blakely message.[22] The lead message was clear: *"Are women lawyers paying enough attention to upward mobility?* Offered opinions that are antithetical to the core beliefs and principles of the American Bar Association."[23]

Refo went on to say that the problem with Blakely's piece was that she blamed the wrong people in the piece: "Blaming women attorneys is appalling."[24] Refo cited *Walking Out the Door,* and the 2020 ABA Report, *In Their Own Words,* as evidence that the systematic gender problems in the profession that have plagued it for generations still persist, through no fault of the women suffering the disparities. "We will not stand by and watch half of the legal profession walk out the door, taking their skills and experience just when they should be at their most effective," she wrote. "That's terrible business for the profession and terrible for clients. And it is wrong."[25]

In an interview with Christina Previte, host of the *Wake Up Call* podcast, Blakely responded to the backlash, stating that she was surprised by the negative reactions, calling it "rather harsh" and unlike anything she'd ever experienced. She argued that she was motivated to write the piece following the pandemic-related global shutdown, as she worried anew about the exodus of women from the law. She was concerned that if women don't keep their seats in the profession, and more specifically, if they don't advance and keep their voices from a "high perch," then they will lack power to change the systemic problems in the profession.[26]

While we take issue with some of Blakely's arguments, we worry, too, about women leaving the law prematurely and the lack of female mentorship at the highest levels of law firm practice. We believe lawyer moms, like any other demographic, can leave the law behind for amazing new careers, if they want to. We also believe that a collaboration between those on the inside and out can really fix what's broken so that more lawyer moms and lawyer caregivers can find their place within the law, without having to leave prematurely.

Should You Walk Out the Door or Not?

A collaboration between ABA and ALM Intelligence, "Walking Out the Door: The Facts, Figures, and Future of Experienced Women Lawyers in Private Practice" by authors Roberta Liebenberg and Stephanie Scharf, focused on the exodus of experienced women from the law who are leaving in much higher numbers than their male counterparts. Among other things, Liebenberg and Scharf noted that this attrition of senior female lawyers creates a vacuum of mentorship for younger female lawyers, a fact that very likely perpetuates the cycle of attrition.

It's true. The numbers speak volumes. More than 50% of law grads are women. Nearly 45% of the incoming associate classes are female. Yet less than 25% end up equity partners.[27] Liebenberg and Scharf ask: "The critical question, of course, is why? What is it about the experiences in Big Law that result in such different outcomes for women than men, and why do even senior women lawyers have so many more obstacles to overcome?"[28]

We believe there can be no doubt that the systemic gender disparity in Big Law is a problem. Consider these reported statistics from the *Walking Out the Door* report:

Percentage of respondents who report having been mistaken for a lower-level employee:
> 82% women
> 0% men

Percentage of respondents who report having experienced demeaning comments, stories, jokes:
> 75% women
> 8% men

Percentage of respondents who report having experienced a lack of access to business development opportunities:
> 67% women
> 10% men

Percentage of respondents who report having been [perceived] less committed to his/her career:

    63% women

    2% men

Percentage of respondents who report having been denied or overlooked for advancement or promotion

    53% women

    7% men

Percentage of respondents who report having missed out on a desirable assignment

    48% women

    11% men

Percentage of respondents who reported unwanted sexual conduct at work

    50% women

    6% men[29]

The above represent chilling statistics about behavior and discrimination inside the law. And yet, when we look closely at the statistics, we see that there is more to change than the systemic gender disparity on the inside.

Considering that this report was issued in 2019, and not 1919, it is stunning that 54% of women say that they are fully responsible for childcare while only 1% of men say the same.[30] Yes, that's right. Read that again. More than half of working female lawyers say that childcare responsibility is their full responsibility and only a negligible percentage of men say the same. If there is no partnership at home, how are women going to forge successful partnerships at their respective law firms?

Furthermore, statistics show that there has been a disparate impact on women in the workplace as a result of the COVID-19 pandemic. And this disparate impact is causing burnout at faster rates among women. For example, the 2021 Women in the Workplace report released by LeanIn.org and McKinsey & Company found that: "One in three women says they have considered down-shifting their careers or leaving the workforce this year, compared to 1 in 4 who said this a few months into the pandemic. Additionally, 4 in 10 women have considered leaving their company or switching jobs—and high employee turnover in recent months suggests that many of them are following through."[31]

Some important reforms have developed in this field, including childcare in the office, concierge services and flexible work hours. While many big law firms have implemented "emergency" child care infrastructure, it's clearly not enough. In an article published in 2017 in *The American Lawyer*, the authors reportedly reached out to several firms including mega-firm (and Amy's former law firm) Skadden Arps to ask why there is no long-term child care infra-structure, but got no answer.[32]

Another consideration for law firms is to be clear that opportunities for flexible and remote work don't lead to a more exaggerated "always on" culture that law firms are notorious for. As the 2021 Women in Workplace Report from McKinsey and Company and LeanIn.org noted: Since the pandemic, almost all employees they spoke to "say they have at least some flexibility to take time off and step away from work. However, more than a third feel like they are expected to be 'always on,' and employees who feel this way are much more likely to say they are often or almost always burned out."[33]

We believe that women on the inside of law should lobby for and demand appropriate child care options, and concierge services and flexible arrangements. Of course, these resources are only successful if sexual harassment and gender stigma considerations are minimized. In other words, written policies are not enough in a law firm culture that is still so overtly biased. Law firms have to commit to promoting women who use the policies in order to reverse the momentum of the stigmas and discrimination.

In sum, caregiver bias persists in the law firm culture, and in many cases creates death by a thousand cuts for female attorneys. Eventually female lawyers and lawyer caregivers may find them-selves worn out and having no choice but to leave the law. Until law firms change their corporate culture, women will continue to leave in droves that perpetuate the cycle. Change will not come solely from those of us outside the law.

Toasting the Sandwich Generation

About 15% of all American adults provide some unpaid care-giving assistance to another adult and many of these caregivers are balancing multi-generational needs.[34] In fact, a 2018 Pew Research Center report estimated that 29% of American adults have a minor child at home and that 12% of these parents also provide unpaid care for another adult as well.[35] The demands on unpaid caregivers' time is increasing and is staggering. In a statistic that may well surprise you, despite the portrayals provided by the media, caregivers today actually spend more time with their children than they did in the 1960s. The Pew Research Center also found that "[t]he amount of time parents spend on child care has been on the rise for decades in the United States. Mothers now spend 40% more time with their kids than they did in the mid-1960s, and the amount of time spent by fathers has tripled during that span."[36] This means that for parents also facing competing multi-generational caregiving, the balance is growing more and more exhausting.

Caregiving for parents and other adults can prove particularly challenging because of the complicated emotions associated with the care. In contrast to raising a child and preparing them to launch into the world, adult caregiving can often trigger fears about aging, mortality, and other anxieties of the caregiver.[37] Health care trends, including shorter hospitalizations and rising insurance costs result in more need for sophisticated and demanding caregiving needs, such as personal care and medical care. And so, while no less rewarding, caring for parents and other adults can be more fraught with stress than caring for minor children. The average age of working caregivers is 49: a peak age for earning capacity and thus, when a caregiver leaves the workforce due to caregiving demands and stressors, the financial loss can be substantial.[38]

Of course, COVID-19 brought new challenges and juggling needs to the Sandwich Generation. Multi-generational caregivers not only had to figure out how to juggle remote work, changing work needs, virtual learning needs of minor children, caregiving needs of older parents, but they also had to figure out how to do all of this without compromising their health or the health of members of the older and more vulnerable populations in their care. The impact and stress of this juggle and other factors had a disproportionate effect on women in the workplace: 4 times as many women than men left the workforce in 2020.[39]

So to you, dear Sandwich Generation, we say: hold on. It's true that we want to help you leave the law if you want to. But we also want to help enact change where change is due.

How Do We Enact Change? Listen

From a bird's-eye view outside of the law, we transitioning lawyers often have lots of ideas of how things should be made better inside the law firm walls. But we must do more. We must listen to the words of those on the inside.

In a 2020 ABA Report, entitled *"In Their Own Words,"* authored by Joyce Sterling and Linda Chanow, we have a chance to do just that.[40] In their report, Sterling and Chanow interviewed focus groups of women both within and outside the law to compare experiences and reactions of both and evaluate some of the reasons that women leave the law in disproportionate numbers to men. The results were startling.

Both women inside and outside the law reported that on a list of things they liked best about practicing law, intellectual stimulation and colleagues were at the top and money was at the bottom.[41] And yet many women inside and outside the law firm environment still reported that the perceived pay disparity between men and women is a pervasive problem in law. It seems that the issue is less about exact dollars, and more about fairness. The measure of compensating partners is reportedly ever-changing, and many women reported differing standards used for them versus their male counterparts. For example, some women reported working reduced hours to accommodate their caregiving, but bringing in as much or more business than male counterparts, and being penalized. They also reported being penalized for other partners' "bad years" while also being asked to prove more than one "good year" whereas male counterparts did not have such exacting standards placed on them.

One particularly egregious example was reported: "Another law firm partner discovered that she was being paid $80,000 a year less than the senior male associates. When she asked for the explanation of the disparity, the senior partner said, "[His] wife is home, and he has to support a wife and kids." When she explained that she was supporting a husband and two kids, the senior partner responded, "Well, your husband can leave and go to work."[42]

The bottom line is that the compensation programs used by firms are still highly subjective and as Sterling and Chanow report are "frequently controlled by the 'old boy' networks that leave women feeling cheated when the credit is handed out. As a result, women are voting with their feet and leaving their firms."

The hyper-competitive atmosphere in the law firm world is also reported as a continuing fatal problem. Colleagues are not working together on a common goal other than to cut each other down and diminish each other's returns.[43] The sexism and racism, both overt and subtle, is devastating in many law firm environments.[44]

All of these factors, and more, combine to force women and caregivers out of the practice of law prematurely, driving them away from a field where they have loved and embraced the intellectual rigor, challenge, and analytical rewards of a law career they started off loving. Is there any other choice?

How about staying in the practice of law, but on your own terms? The story of Big Law attorney, Tara, Partner and Director of Pro Bono Services at her firm, is instructional, as she has done just that. Tara has managed to carve out a path to success and partnership in her law firm by staying in the law, on her own terms. After graduating from law school, clerking, and then entering the legal practice, she quickly identified some of the same fatal flaws in the law firm culture that we've been reporting here. But Tara decided that instead of leaving the practice of law entirely, she'd practice law on her own terms, with intellectually stimulating work that would serve to create a more collegial atmosphere in her firm rather than diminish it. To that end, she created a program to enhance the *pro bono* work and, in turn, profile, of her firm. She was made partner and continues to work largely on *pro bono* work for the firm, receiving multiple awards for her work, and managing to cultivate what she reports as fulfilling work, alongside her roles as wife and multi-generational caregiver as well.

What if more women worked to create the space they want in law? What if, even better, more women *worked together* to create the space they want in law? These would include spaces where fairness and parity are prioritized. Where lawyers lifted each other up and supported each other toward a common coal of enhanced legal practice for their colleagues and clients, rather than working to cut each other down.

Tara notes that she takes an approach that some might consider unusual in Big Law: she is honest and vocal about the struggles and the joys of being a working parent. She tries to bond with other male and female colleagues by embracing her identity as lawyer and caregiver inside the office and out.

Says Tara, "I don't shy away from it. I talk about it, and I find it is a way to open up dialogue and for all of us to view each other as human beings. What is interesting is that it has helped me to create good bonds with some of the toughest male partners, who open up and share things about their families and their experience with being a parent. And certainly it isn't just with parenting. It is with a common love of dogs, sports teams, travel, Peloton, etc.; but I find [sharing my whole self] helps me to get to know attorneys at my firm, clients, and even opposing counsel. The sharing helps collegiality all around."

And what if all of this collegiality resulted in better outcomes for clients, and more cost-effective legal services, resulting in an increase in demand, and a larger volume of business for those law firms who made it their business to practice this way? Is it too aspirational to hope that this way of practicing law could actually replace the old boys' ways?

We don't think so. Listen, for example, to the words of lawyer and mom, Laura French, who believes we can still change the law from the inside, and she has done exactly that, albeit on her own terms. She's so passionate about her vocation, she's trademarked her moniker, The Mom Lawyer®, and is still a practicing lawyer, as founder and owner of the successful firm, French Law Group, LLC, focusing on estate planning, business strategies, and intellectual property law.

French calls The Mom Lawyer® brand genesis "truly a lightning bolt and a 'feather thought.'" She goes on to explain: "A feather thought is one of those things that crosses your mind that you immediately know is true and important. The idea for The Mom Lawyer® popped into my head one evening. I was working with a coach/consultant at the time, and my son William was young. I was thinking about the unique insights that I bring to the table. It occurred to me that I had been, for my entire career, a mom of sorts to my clients. And I was an actual mom to one precious soul. Voila, The Mom Lawyer®."

French shares insights on balancing caregiving with work, demonstrating that perhaps it's less about "juggling" and more about "integrating." "This [work/caregiving balance] is a timely subject in my family. We've experienced a significant medical crisis, with a series of smaller events within the crisis. I've been able to jump in and manage some of the crisis since I can control my own schedule. Because of my practice area, I also have insight into the types of programs and benefits available through public programs or community resources ... I have used my own family's experience to reflect upon how I can better serve and support my clients who come to me with similar circumstances."

French notes, too, the gender disparity pressures from outside the law firm that unfortunately influence caregivers within the law. "From a societal standpoint, women are expected to put others first. We are taught to sacrifice self for our children, spouses, parents, community, friends. These beliefs are slowly changing, and I hope that women and men will recognize the unreasonable expectations that women have shouldered for so very long. We cannot bring home the bacon and fry it up in a pan. Superwoman is an unattainable standard."

But French also argues that women cannot take a passive role in expecting these societal norms to change. Lawyers in training learn much about briefing cases, analyzing precedent and crafting compelling arguments. But there is perhaps an important missing piece in the training that should be considered. She says, "Law school doesn't teach us to collaborate and champion one another. I believe it takes a lot of personal growth and development to reach a place where you don't view your sister-in-the-law as a threat, but as colleague, someone you can learn from and also teach. If you're lucky enough and are vulnerable with people who have earned the right to hear your story (thank you Brene Brown), you'll find some sisters who will challenge and cheer you."

Refuse to Cease and Desist

Michelle Browning Coughlin, founder of MothersEsquire, a nonprofit organization that advocates for gender equity, motherhood, and caregiver issues in the legal profession, describes how "motherhood was always part of the journey." She had both of her children while still in law school, and still managed to reach #1 in her class, and secure a coveted large firm offer following law school. But she realized that despite her drive, her successful legal career, and her work ethic, she was still viewed with skepticism by her non-parenting peers. One lawyer said to her, "I wasn't sure about you, with the kids and all." The pressure to be a supermom and superlawyer felt like a "cage" she was trying to break free from.

Michelle made it her mission to seek out other like-minded associates, and mobilize them into action. She did it through a

Facebook group at first, and has grown the brand to include community advocacy and a concerted effort to help lawyer moms find their voices. She has no intention of leaving the law, but she's sure going to help people leave the law's stigma against working parents and especially lawyer moms.

We believe that recent movements in the law firm realm, like French's The Mom Lawyer® and MothersEsquire, are beacons of hope for women lawyers and lawyer caregivers in general. And they are not merely aspirational tools, as evidenced by the unique firms and concrete communities they've helped create and mobilize. The fact that the ABA has been willing and active to sponsor research that helps shine a spotlight on these issues (including the four-part report series that includes *Walking Out the Door* and *In Their Own Voices*) provides credible evidence that the industry itself is reflecting and open to change.

While we will always advocate for those lawyers who are ready to transition away from the law, we will continue to support those trying to improve law firm culture from the inside out so that no lawyer in transition will ever have to question whether she has made the right decision at the right time, but rather will be able to embrace a new chapter with zeal and enthusiasm.

CHAPTER 3

Approaching the Exit Ramp: A Break or a Break-up?

"I'd do the things I wanted to do when I was 12. I think everyone should think about what they wanted to do when they were 12. Look back to what magazines they were reading, what they were imagining, and pretty much go and do that."[45]

–Andrew Comrie-Picard, NYC Big Law survivor turned professional race and stunt car driver

Hostage or Partnership Material?

IN 2009, IN A SMALL TOWN IN KANSAS (Dover, population 1,700), following a high-speed chase involving patrol cars and a helicopter, Jessee Dimmick ran a stolen minivan up onto the front yard of Jared and Lindsay Rowley.[46] Jared thought the commotion he was watching out his window was a traffic accident until he heard four gunshots, at which point he told Lindsay to go hide in the basement. Dimmick let himself inside the Rowley's house and offered Jared Rowley a sum of money (the amount was disputed, but might have been up to $10,000) to help him hide from the police. Jared apparently tried to convince Dimmick to leave, and even tried to push him out the door, but Dimmick pointed to a pocketknife in his pocket, and told Rowley, "Man, you don't want to do this." Ultimately, Lindsay came out of hiding and the couple gave Dimmick food and clothes, let him stay in the house, and watched movies with him, all in the hopes that he wouldn't hurt them. Eventually, he fell asleep, the couple escaped, and the SWAT team arrived to arrest Dimmick.

End of story? Not quite. Dimmick was tried and convicted of kidnapping, felony theft, and eluding the police. The appellate court later affirmed, but while his appeal was pending, and in response to the Rowley's civil suit against Dimmick, Dimmick countersued for breach of contract. In his pleadings, Dimmick stated: "I, the defendant, asked the Rowleys to hide me because I feared for my life. I offered the Rowleys an unspecified amount of money which they agreed upon, therefore forging a legally binding oral contract."

The Rowleys objected to the suit, claiming there could be no breach of contract since there was no meeting of the minds, no agreement on essential terms, and even if there was some agreement as to the partnership, it was made under duress. The trial judge agreed with the Rowleys and dismissed Dimmick's claim on motion.

The *Dimmick/Rowley* case has been held out and cited as one of the most ridiculous lawsuits ever filed. Maybe so. But one could argue that Dimmick wasn't so crazy after all to think the Kansas bar might understand his plight.

After all, what professionals other than lawyers routinely agree to often intolerable environments for the promise of partnership and cash?

Exposing a Culture of Unwellness

One of the biggest hurdles to developing healthy exit strategies from the practice of law is also one of reasons many want to leave in the first place: the culture of unwellness that pervades the profession. It is true that at any given time in any career you may feel overwhelmed, stressed, and anxious. In the law, these feelings are common. But more than that, they are expected, rationalized, and, in some cases, cultivated by the archaic protocols of a profession that still believes that the person who works the most hours (and sleeps the least) and takes none of their vacation days or weekends off wins.

Historically there has been little recognition given to the effects of this culture on lawyers. A 2016 study funded by the American Bar Association (ABA) Commission on Lawyer Assistance Programs and the Hazelden Betty Ford Foundation surveyed 13,000 practicing lawyers ("2016 ABA/Betty Ford Study"), noting:

> For too long, the legal profession has turned a blind eye to widespread health problems. Many in the legal profession have behaved, at best, as if their colleagues' well-being is none of their business. At worst, some appear to believe that supporting well-being will harm professional success. Many also appear to believe that lawyers' health problems are solely attributable to their own personal failings for which they are solely responsible.[47]

The side effects of a profession whose culture at best ignores and at worst encourages unwellness have been staggering. That same 2016 ABA/Betty Ford Study found that between 21 and 36 percent of practicing lawyers may qualify as problem drinkers, and that approximately 28 percent, 19 percent, and 23 percent are struggling with some level of depression, anxiety, and stress, respectively.[48]

If you're thinking this unwellness is limited to seasoned lawyers only, think again. The 2016 ABA/Betty Ford Study found that the highest rates of drinking problems and depression were actually in the youngest lawyers: those in their first ten years of practice and those in private firms. By the way, the surveyed lawyers without reported substance or mental health issues were hardly *happy*. High numbers in that category still reported that career satisfaction was lacking.[49]

Following the release of the 2016 ABA/Betty Ford Study, a coalition of entities both within and outside the American Bar Association convened to form the National Task Force on Lawyer Well Being, and a report was issued in 2017 ("2017 Task Force Report") with recommendations in an attempt to address the demonstrable unwellness among practicing lawyers, remove the stigma for seeking help, and create a path for continued evaluation and growth within the profession.[50] The 2017 Task Force Report defined "lawyer well-being" in the following way:

"A continuous process whereby lawyers seek to thrive in each of the following areas: emotional health, occupational pursuits, creative or intellectual endeavors, sense of spirituality or greater purpose in life, physical health, and social connections with others. Lawyer well-being is part of a lawyer's ethical duty of competence. It includes lawyers' ability to make healthy, positive work/life choices to assure not only a quality of life within their families and communities, but also to help them make responsible decisions for their clients. It includes maintaining their own long-term well-being."[51]

The 2017 Task Force Report takes a sober and brutally honest approach, noting that:

Historically, law firms, law schools, bar associations, courts, and malpractice insurers have taken a largely hands-off approach to these issues. They have dealt with them only when forced to because of impairment that can no longer be ignored. The dedication and hard work of lawyer assistance programs aside, we have not done enough to help, encourage, or require lawyers to be, get, or stay well. However, the goal of achieving increased lawyer well-being is within our collective reach. The time to redouble our efforts is now.[52]

Interestingly, there is evidence that the issues rampant throughout the legal profession may often begin as early as law school.

Law students start law school with high life satisfaction and strong mental health measures. But within the first year of law school, they experience a significant increase in anxiety and depression. Research suggests that law students are among the most dissatisfied, demoralized, and depressed of any graduate student population.[53]

So how to address the declining mental state of lawyers as they start and continue their training? Most state bar admission agencies require truthful questions about candidates' mental health as part of the fitness and qualification process. There is noted tension between camps that believe this is a necessary way of maintaining the integrity of the profession and those that believe such a requirement actually stigmatizes mental health issues and stunts voluntary treatment efforts. The Task Force recommendation is that there be a shift away from questions of diagnosis and treatment and instead include a slate of more focused questions to mental qualities/conditions that could affect the practice of law. There is an argument, however, that this is a distinction without substance, and that so long as the legal profession continues to put its members on the chopping block for admitting to health issues, the profession simply cannot thrive.

Of course, social support is a key component to combatting the mental health strains of the profession, and the arguably meager social support present inside the profession has been significantly eroded during the pandemic. Law firms have been criticized for being among the first workplaces that have returned to live work models post-pandemic, and the question remains whether post-pandemic law firms can provide innovative forward-thinking social support systems with live work models, or whether their return-to-work plans are focused solely on the bottom line.

Hold on a minute. But isn't that fiscally prudent? To focus on the bottom line? Not really. The Task Force Report noted the irony of bottom line-driven corporate cultures is that it leads to depression and anxiety, which in turn *affects the bottom line*. In reality, the push to return to live work models without proper support, and the inability of the profession to grow and progress, creates more attrition, leaving work burdens to reshuffle among fewer people. This creates burnout, which creates more attrition, and so on.

This type of revolving door culture keeps the cycle alive in which an "easy" access to lucrative work continues to exist for law students lulling them (and their law schools seeking accreditation and high rankings) into a pattern in which arguably more reward-ing and more creative work is not sought out. Essentially, the Task Force recommends a shift in culture from one that rewards unreasonable expectations, deadlines, and lack of autonomy to one that incorporates more feedback and support from law school to law firm.

We agree and fully support such a shift! But until that happens, it might be necessary to self-monitor. Kudos to the firms who have taken a hard look at what they can do to help remedy the pervasive culture of unwellness and stop glorifying it, and shame on those who haven't yet gotten on board. We leave the task of cleaning up the practice to others and applaud their efforts. In the meantime, we focus on helping attorneys caught up in the culture of unwell-ness, recognize it and escape from it, where desired.

Listen, we'd like to think that eventually the idea of staying in an oppressive law firm environment will be considered just as ridiculous as, say, suing your hostages for calling the cops on you. If you're with us here, and you're nodding along, the next sentence is either going to seem difficult to process or life-saving. The truth is it's both.

Our friends, it's time for a break.

In many ways, leaving the practice of law can resemble any other kind of relationship breakup. The comparisons include emotional trauma, financial implications, and other practical con-siderations.

Amy readily concedes that her exodus from Skadden Arps—and from the practice of law entirely after a 13-year corporate litigation career—actually prepared her for divorce a decade later. The identity issues and grief she navigated when leaving her Big Law gig behind were pretty good landmarks for the road she'd travel down later after a 24-year marriage ended, and she credits her resiliency following her divorce in large part to the healing process she'd gone through during and immediately following her breakup with the law.

In fact, we've canvassed messages of the top thought leaders in the areas of relationship counseling and found that much of the same advice relating to ending personal relationships is relevant in this space as well.

Psychotherapist and New York Times bestselling author Esther Perel says that when evaluating whether it's time to leave, there are four key signs that signal that a relationship is effectively over: indifference, neglect, contempt, and violence. Violence in this context, Perel claims, can take the form of microaggressions, which makes her model spot on for evaluating whether it's time to take a break from the law as well.[54]

Clinical psychologist and researcher Dr. Antonio Pascual-Leone believes there's a three-step sequence that marks the end of all relationships, whether personal or business.[55] He advises, first, that you allow yourself to tolerate the distress and discomfort, and learn how to articulate what hurts the most about ending the relationship. Next, deal with the older, uglier feelings that this particular goodbye brings up and ask yourself what you need to move forward even if—and this is particularly relevant in the case of a professional transition—even if you don't feel entitled to it. Finally, Dr. Pascual-Leone advises that following a break-up, the last step is to emerge from the anger and grief by asserting yourself in a healthy way.

The takeaway? Breaking up with the law might be just the solution to continue a lawyer's personal quest for well-being, but breaking up with the law can also be a lot like breaking up with a partner or leaving behind other personal relationships. If you do decide to make a more permanent break, you'll need to focus on cultivating resilience and risk tolerance (which we talk about in more detail in Chapter 5).

As with personal relationships, the ultimate divorce from the law might actually follow a long separation, and maybe even a period of small breaks while you try out life on your own. After all, as we talk to interrupted lawyers of all demographics and walks of life, the universal message is that you cannot really understand, in a practical, concrete way, the opportunities available to a person with your expertise and background until you step away from the practice of law. And yet, the uncertainty of any other possible opportunity keeps many lawyers stuck in their current place of dissatisfaction and grief. It's a vicious cycle that keeps many would-be transitioning lawyers stuck where they are, and ultimately unhappy.

How to break the cycle? The same advice that relationship experts give in personal matters applies here: Don't be afraid to be vulnerable (Thank you, Brene Brown); Learn how to accept joy without leaning into fear (Many thanks, Brene Brown); Trust your inner voice (Amen, Glennon Doyle). And ultimately, as Esther Perel cautions, sometimes you have to find yourself through separation. Frankly, you might find that a short sabbatical actually helps you reconnect with your original passion for the law. Maybe it even helps refuel it. Either way, you'll never unlock the benefits that can be gained by a break (or break-up) until you try.

Yes, You CAN Take a Break. Here's How.

When you think about it for long enough, which we have, there's a good chance you'll see that if the law firm culture you're currently in is toxic, the best way out, is, well, out.

How long of a break should you take? Simple. *As much as you need.* Thank you very much, COVID.

At this point, we want to reiterate that we understand there are large sectors of the workforce who cannot and should not take a break of any length. Of course, there are socioeconomic factors at play that are best left for another discussion. Here, we are talking about unhappy lawyers, and not comparing them to essential workers such as medical personnel or first responders. If you have had COVID or lost someone to COVID, the notion that COVID has taught us lessons about taking a break from work may seem insensitive. We do not mean to compound your suffering. We are focusing here on those who have suffered a different kind of loss in the pandemic, one of identity and economics. COVID survivors and grievers, our intention is not to minimize or dismiss your trauma in any way.

In 2020, in the midst of the global pandemic and lockdown, we wrote about the silver linings provided by COVID.[56] We still feel those silver linings are very real, and in fact, we see even more. For one thing, COVID has introduced flexibility into our workspace and lives and changed the way we work forever. While law firms and legal settings were one of the first workplace cultures to demand a return to live face-to-face workplaces, we have still seen technological advances find a new home in the legal workspaces (at the very least, with the introduction of Zoom and virtual work and meetings, we've reduced some travel). And while it's clear to us that lawyers will never give up working in real life settings, it is also clear that we now have that thing available to us in our schedule that we've always claimed we needed: time. With the mainstream acceptance of Zoom and virtual meetings as part of the hybrid workplace culture, we have more flexibility in our schedules to explore alternatives to the law.

Put simply, *you* have the flexibility your pre-COVID practicing ancestors didn't have, in order to take a variety of completely socially acceptable breaks ranging from a good night's sleep to a year-long sabbatical. Which one is right for you?

Iffy Ibekwe, principal attorney and founder of Ibekwe Law, PLLC, makes one of the best cases for taking a break from the practice of law with just a good night's sleep that we've heard. She has been able to use this philosophy to remain in active practice for over a decade. Reminding us that "most people need six to nine hours of quality sleep to reduce stress levels, lower cortisol, and allow the body to heal," Ibekwe advocates for regular uninterrupted sleep at any cost, including advocating for a sleep consultant, based on personal experience.[57]

Need something a little heartier than one good night's sleep? Spoiler alert: yes, you do. Consider this breakthrough idea: take your weekends off. Ok. We are willing to dial back on that completely extreme idea. But can you give us a Saturday or two a month? And if yes, can you *schedule* them? In other words, can you use them as part of your maybe-exit-strategy rather than letting them disappear in a wasteland of sleep catch-up and self-medicating?

What was that? A maybe? Good, we'll take it. Here's what you do with your four Saturdays off a month for the next six months. (Ok, ok. We'll take your counter-offer. Whatever it is. Can't blame us for trying to negotiate the maximum. We are lawyers, after all.) Use your Saturdays off as real, actual breaks. Schedule them ahead of time. Ease into them with a good night's sleep on Friday, or the best you can muster. Be cautious about the use of sleep aids and consult with a physician for the best sleep plan rather than self-medicating. Schedule your days off as stringently as you schedule your days *on.*

Add yoga, meditation, a workout, pleasure reading, and/or other relaxation time into the day. Plan for healthy food ahead of time. Consider scheduling a grocery delivery or a healthy takeout option ahead of time to prevent meal decisions from consuming your valuable day off, or worse, causing you to abandon healthy eating decisions altogether.

Oh, and another thing: do a project. Says Gretchen Rubin, New York Times bestselling author of *The Happiness Project*: "Happier people have control." So, give yourself a project with a beginning, middle, end. Why do you think so many people turned to closet-cleaning and bread-baking during the pandemic?[58]

The most important thing is to schedule a block of time on the day off to explore (either via computer research, a lunch meeting, a Zoom meeting, or otherwise) at least one alternative career to the practice of law. Keep a journal or google document with your observations, findings, and questions.

And how will you know if you're doing this right? If you're being as productive as possible with your time off? Easy, you'll want more of it. You might be able to work up to all four of those Saturdays per month, and you might—we realize this is a leap but we are cautiously optimistic—want to start taking some of that unused vacation time as well. Eventually, you'll have a directory of resources outside your lawyer circle that you can consult as you evaluate whether a longer break is in order.

The best part about this plan outlined above? It's completely risk-averse, and thus lawyer-friendly. And frankly, nearly fail-proof. Exploring alternatives to legal careers while still remaining in the practice is one of the surest ways to succeed at a transition from the practice of law should you decide a transition is for you. (And if you decide it isn't? Well, you haven't lost anything except a couple of Saturdays at the office.)

As Amy discussed in *Lawyer Interrupted,* unless you are independently wealthy or do not have to work, you may have to be prepared to pursue your alternative career choice on the side for a while. The story of internationally acclaimed Lego brick artist, Nathan Sawaya, has become a model illustration for the successful transitioning attorney. Nathan worked on art six hours per night, every night, after he came home from his Manhattan law firm job for several years before he transitioned to a professional artist. Sawaya was arguably ahead of his time in 2003 and 2004. At a time when "web logs" or "blogs" were brand new, particularly in the art industry, he set up an art blog, showing off the creations he was making at night after long hours at his Manhattan corporate law firm. He was receiving website hits, and some professional commissions, but one day in 2004, when his website crashed from so many hits, he began to think that maybe he had enough interest in his art to pursue it as a viable career. He left his corporate career at Winston & Strawn soon after and never looked back.

There are other less dramatic examples of crashing websites, of course. (We discuss many of them in Chapter 12). And it is a necessary truism that your website will not crash unless you are actively maintaining one. You must be cultivating interests, hobbies, and/or potential alternative careers to recognize the moment when you just might be able to make one such activity your new career.

We may not be able to make a clean break from the law overnight, but we can incorporate virtual meetings and experiences into our schedules. We can join Boards. We can do volunteer work. We can network like crazy.

In a word, yes. COVID was a forced break for all of us. And if there's anything COVID taught us, it was that time is relative. In the early weeks of the national shutdown in March and April 2020, we thought we couldn't last one more day in isolation, masked and short on toilet paper. Of course one year later, with surging cases and a vaccine finally available but only in limited quantities, those early weeks of quarantine felt like child's play.

Was it the break you needed?

If yes, good for you. But if you're reading this, we suspect it was not. And as you explore the Saturday off method, you may well decide that's all you need to rejuvenate and find your way back to productivity and a career in the law that fulfills you. You may find that you can reframe and recharge without succumbing to a pervasive culture of unwellness.

But if not, if you're still feeling like it's time to make a break—*more of a break*—then let us make the case for extreme measures. Time and time again, we hear from successfully transitioning lawyers that you can't get true perspective until you get away. True clarity requires some period of disconnect. Take your vacation days!

And if you're ready for more, take a sabbatical. A six-month or one-year break from the law can be a productive, fairly risk averse way of testing the waters outside the practice if you outline some parameters ahead of time with your firm. You might feel that you can't take a sabbatical right now during these uncertain times. But consider this: Amy actually took her life-changing sabbatical from the law at another completely uncertain time, in 2009, in the aftermath of the Lehman Brothers collapse and subsequent recession.

At that time, Skadden Arps opened applications to a sabbatical program known as "Sidebar Plus" as a way of saving money and helping some attorneys self-select out during a challenging time for the firm; it was a way to avoid massive layoffs and bad publicity. Amy's initial sabbatical application was denied; her department chair responded when she applied for a sabbatical, "Absolutely not. You're a litigator, not an M&A attorney, and you're too busy to leave." Amy negotiated her sabbatical by arguing that she'd write about the sabbatical and bring some good PR to the firm (which she did) and also argued that shifting not-so-busy M&A attorneys into litigation positions might be a good way to respond to the disproportional sabbatical applications by litigators (which Skadden did). The bottom line is that it might seem that you don't have much bargaining power, but you do. It's more cost effective for the firm to welcome you back after six months or a year than to hire and train a new attorney. And an economically challenging time might be the perfect time to convince your firm that a partially subsidized sabbatical is a sound way to save some money. You'll never know until you ask.

Making Your Time off Work for You

No matter how long of a break you take from the law, it's important to make that time work for you. Think about it. If you won a sum of money, you wouldn't just stuff that cash under your mattress, would you? You'd invest it, or deposit it into an interest-bearing account, or you'd do *something to make sure that money worked for you.*

Your time is valuable and so your break from the law should be treated in the same way. Use the time to cultivate a network, hone new skills, and master new channels of social media.

To this end, the story of Alli Elmunzer is compelling. Alli is an attorney-turned-entrepreneur who then became a successful attorney *for entrepreneurs.* After leaving law school, traveling a fairly traditional route, and landing in a law firm, practicing commercial real estate, Alli became dissatisfied with law firm life. At the time, Alli decided that satisfaction must mean she didn't actually like the law.

With an eye toward an exit strategy, Alli started exploring ways to monetize her passion: photography. Noting that the barrier to entry of the photography profession was fairly low, she started a website, secured some initial photography clients on the side of her law firm practice, and soon left the law entirely to pursue a growing commercial photography business.

But Alli quickly realized that she could hone her business skills (first explored through her undergraduate degree) and learn about running a business. She also quickly learned that she could assemble a network of fellow creative entrepreneurs who had a need she could fill: legal advice from an attorney-turned-entrepreneur.

Soon, Alli's break from the law became an on-road back to the law as she started Influencer Legal, a niche legal practice for small businesses, with a focus on women entrepreneurs needing help with trademark, brand, and other intellectual property issues. Because her practice is so specific, Alli has been able to successfully market through social media avenues, including Clubhouse and Instagram, and by her fourth year of business, was poised to expand, with growth plans including the hiring of an operations manager.

Alli later realized that it wasn't the law she wanted to leave, but rather the traditional routes offered to law school students that would have you believe Big Law is the only real avenue after graduation. By taking an exit ramp from the law, Alli discovered another world was available to her. She also discovered how to create and grow a small business, translatable skills as she returned to the solo practice of law (itself a brand-new entrepreneurial venture for Alli!) to help others learn how to successfully create and grow *their* own small businesses. In this way, Alli's exit ramp actually led to a full circle journey, albeit with a much more satisfying destination this time around.

Exit Ramp Advice From an Actual Professional Driver

"It sounds so corny, but just go through the first door. You'll never see the other opportunities—the subsequent doors to open—until you start down the path."[59] So says Andrew Comrie-Picard, former litigator turned professional race and stunt car driver.[60] Comrie-Picard obtained his law degree from McGill and went on to work in New York City Big Law while still continuing to pursue an early passion, racing, alongside practicing law. Eventually, this professional driver (with film credits in the *Fast & Furious* franchise and *Deadpool 2*) saw a viable exit ramp, and took it. His story is unique and yet familiar, in that he pursued an alternative career alongside his law career, allowing the law to subsidize and help fuel his next chapter as a race car driver (no pun intended!).

"[T]he fact is that the alternative to law just chose me: I ended up spending enough time on the racing that there just wasn't enough room for a law career, too. Fortunately, the income from the nascent law career helped launch my racing career, so I can't really say it could have been done another way." Ultimately, when he decided to make a break from the law, it was to avoid a life of regret. "I decided 'I better give this a go' because I didn't want to regret missing out on my dream. And it all worked out because, in truth, I was a terrible lawyer."[61]

Whether you're a terrible lawyer or not, are you convinced you need a break? (Or at least more convinced than you were when you started this chapter?) Maybe now you're asking, WHERE do I start? And WHEN do I start?

We'll help you with that in the chapters to come. But first, let's talk about addressing that thing you already know you're going to struggle with: an identity crisis. Let's nip that in the bud, shall we?

CHAPTER 4

The Identity Crisis: How to Leave Your Legal Career Without Losing Yourself in the Process

"I did not really care what anybody thought when I decided that I didn't want to be a lawyer anymore."[62]

—Risa Weaver-Enion, lawyer turned wedding planner

YOU MAY BE THINKING, "I can't leave the law. Who would I be, if I were not a lawyer?" In this chapter, we'll talk about how to rediscover and maintain your sense of identity and purpose while developing a critical distance from the legal profession.

As lawyers, we are trained to spot and be hypersensitive to risk. The risks of leaving the law can seem too overwhelming even to think about, let alone to assess in the systematic way that we are trained to do. So let us help you with that. While the risks of leaving the law can appear enormous at first, looking at each of them closely can help deflate the fears that unhappy lawyers associate with developing a sensible exit strategy.

For many lawyers, a major barrier to leaving is the fear of giving up a prestigious job. After all, if you have been practicing law with any degree of success, whether at a large firm or a small practice, most people would view you as an achiever. Law is often seen as an impressive field, a challenging and financially rewarding profession that relatively few people can enter. Getting through law school, passing one or more bar exams, and becoming a lawyer make someone part of a relatively high-status and often insular culture. It looks so impressive from the outside.

That is especially so given the ways lawyers and law practice are portrayed on television and in movies. Litigators stride around the courtroom in designer suits, making flawless arguments and decimating witnesses, without so much as a manila folder to structure their work. In popular culture, lawyers ask incisive questions that reveal the truth, and use their powerful intellect and enormous charm to make sure justice is done. They live in glamorous apartments and meet in bars the night before every hearing.

The question you might fear other people asking is: who in their right mind would want to walk away from that?

It can be hard to contemplate leaving the law because that might require admitting to something that many lawyers don't want to think about. One of the most difficult parts of leaving the law is admitting that you are unhappy. "Am I happy?" can seem like a ridiculous, superfluous question. After all, lawyers don't often have time to think about luxuries like happiness because law practice can be so all consuming.

What About the Money?

Losing income during a career change can be a major concern. If you are making a good living, paying your mortgage, student debt, children's school fees, or any of the other prices of modern life, it can be daunting to risk even a minimal disruption of that income stream. Fortunately, there are useful strategies to help minimize the impact of that loss of income.

When contemplating a big drop in income, you can do several things to make sure you remain financially secure. All of these steps are easier to take if you can do them in your own time. Making a career change is not something we suggest doing suddenly or on a whim. We have spoken with plenty of former lawyers who quit their jobs without a plan because they just couldn't take it anymore. While we can identify with their frustration levels, we do not recommend a sudden exit as a strategy. Give yourself as much time as you can to lay the financial groundwork for your exit.

One of the most important steps to take is to look at the resources you have. This should include savings, investments, and cash in emergency accounts. Determining your net worth has to be done in relation to expenses, however. Fixed expenses include things like repaying any student loan debt you may still have, how much you have to pay for your mortgage or rent, and your other monthly living expenses. Therapy expenses and child care expenses are two expenses many transitioning lawyers fail to account for but we think that's a mistake. While you might well be able to reduce child care expenses substantially as you are transitioning, we'd recommend reconsidering before reducing to zero. Getting a sense of how many months you could live on your savings will help you develop a reasonable sense of how long you can go without your current income. During the time you spend planning your exit, you can start putting away even more money in an "escape" or emergency fund if necessary.

Although experts typically recommend setting aside three to six months' worth of expenses, we don't think that is enough for lawyers. The delta between many law firm salaries and other salaries can be significant at first. In fact, while many of the transitioning lawyers we speak to express zero regret about leaving, many do express regret that they didn't save quite enough money first. The idea that a complete career change can be accomplished, a new job started, and living expenses adjusted if necessary within a three-to-six month period may be overly optimistic for many people, although we have certainly seen it happen. And career transitions generally take longer than finding a new job that is similar to an old job. There is research to do, people to persuade (certainly employers, but possibly friends and family as well). We would suggest putting aside at least six to twelve months of living expenses before walking away from your law job.

Once you have determined your financial resources, you can

start reducing your expenses in smaller ways, which could make your next egg last even longer. The time you start considering a potential change is as good a time as any to start finding ways to live on a bit less. Could you cook more often and go out to eat less often? Are there other expenses you can cut down on in the interest of a longer-term investment in your happiness?

Some people find it easy to be relatively frugal. That may be a lifestyle they adopted when they were law students, spending as little as possible, or it may be the way they were brought up (Liz is that way for both reasons). Other people find it more difficult to reduce their discretionary spending. The good news here is that many people find that their expenses naturally go down when they stop working incredibly long hours at a job they don't like. That is not just because they can be home for more meals. It is also because they stop buying things as an act of self-soothing. If a significant part of your monthly credit card bill is made up of impulse purchases, and those impulses are related to work-induced misery, you are likely to make fewer of those purchases when you are more satisfied in other areas of your life.

One expense that may be less fixed than you think is private school tuition. If you are paying full tuition for your children's private school and lose part or all of your income, one of the first steps you should take is to talk with the financial aid office to see if it can offer some assistance. Many parents don't think of this as a source of flexibility, but it can be a great relief to learn that financial aid may be available for parents whose employment circumstances change.

While it might seem a drastic measure, housing costs are often a viable source for reduction. Downsizing your home, or even moving to a nearby, less expensive neighborhood might reduce your financial burdens significantly. Amy recalls the move from New York to Pennsylvania when she left the law as raising quite a few eyebrows; in fact, though, it lowered her cost of living by at least half.

Remember the Hearsay Rule? Don't Rely Too Much on Unreliable Statements

Amy recalls her last day at Skadden when a luncheon was held for the attorneys who had been accepted into the pioneering "Sidebar Plus" sabbatical program. In a posh dining room in the Times Square office building, a veteran partner stood and addressed the group to wish them well and to forecast the future: "You'll be back. And here's why. The most interesting and the most talented people you're ever going to meet are right here in this building. See you in a year."

Says Amy, "I remember thinking: *Really? Is that really true?*" She returned to her office to finish out the day's billable hours, and when a colleague stopped by who wasn't taking a sabbatical and thus, wasn't at the luncheon, she shared the partner's toast with him.

Amy's colleague, whom she thought very highly of, responded, "Well, that's probably true, don't you think?" Amy realized then, that while the veteran partner's toast could not possibly be a reliable statement, certainly everyone in her law firm seemed to *think* it was the truth. This notion that lawyers (particularly Big Law lawyers) are the smartest, and most talented and the best, is a bias she sought to overcome during her sabbatical.

Maybe you also worry that if you leave the law, you won't ever feel as challenged or smart or successful again. But be wary about relying on information you've gleaned from your fellow lawyers in the practice of law. Let's look at some facts and figures.

In a recent U.S. News & World Report on the "Best Jobs," Law actually ranked below Information Security Analyst, Nurse Practitioner, Physician's Assistant, Medical and Health Services Manager, Software Developer, Data Scientist, Financial Planner and Statistician.[63] The criteria for evaluating these so-called "Best Jobs" include: Median Salary, Unemployment Rate, 10-Year Growth Volume, 10-Year Growth Percentage, Future Job Prospects, Stress Level, and Work-Life Balance. Criteria not considered include:

suicide rates, depression rates, and actual hourly rates versus reported salaries. Lawyers do not fare well when these sorts of statistics are considered.[64]

And yes, lawyers' earning capacity is high. But it's not the highest. The same US News & World report found that law was actually #19 on the Best Paying Jobs list, after a number of healthcare-related fields, financial managers, petroleum engineers, marketing managers, and IT managers.[65] And considering the debt-to-income ratio of most lawyers[66], this, too, is a statistic that can be interpreted in various ways.

Interestingly, public perception about lawyers continues to be a mixed bag. The notorious subjects of various jokes, lawyers seem to have built up armor against such heckling by convincing themselves they are among the best and brightest and well-paid professionals. But the public perception of lawyers includes some of the following statistics:

- In a 2015 Gallup poll, only 4% of respondents rated the "honesty and ethical standards" of lawyers as "very high."

- In the same Gallup poll, more than one-third (34%) rated attorneys' honesty and ethical standards as low (25%) or very low (9%).

- An American Bar Association study found that 74% of those surveyed agreed that "lawyers are more interested in winning than in seeing that justice is served."

- That same ABA study found that 69% believed "lawyers are more interested in making money than in serving their clients" and more than half (51%) agreed that "we would be better off with fewer lawyers."[67]

- Forbes recently reported a list of the most and least trusted professions, with lawyers ranking near the bottom, just above business executives and lobbyists.[68]

But wait, you might wonder. Why should we leave the law if those on the outside of law hate us? Well, that's just the thing. When you leave the law, you take the clout of having a law degree and substantial legal training, which is indeed respected by the public, and join fields with significantly more respect, in many cases, than the legal field. A recent look by a Reuters legal columnist at lawyers who have left the profession noted that "Across the board, they all said they were now happier. Poorer perhaps, but happier."[69]

The inherent bias, then, that we often use to justify our perception that in general, lawyers who remain lawyers are superior to other professions, turns out to be unfounded. Be careful about using such unreliable information to make your next move.

Responding to Negative Reactions

One of the hardest parts of making a substantial career shift is dealing with the reactions of other people. Being a lawyer is such a socially acceptable and often prestigious choice. Leaving the law is not: at least, not yet. If going to law school was something your parents encouraged or supported, financially or otherwise, then you may be concerned that they won't support your decision to walk away from a more traditional and stable law path. Even the most well-meaning friends may not know how to be supportive when they learn that you are making a change, especially if they don't understand why you would give up something that often looks great from the outside. Fellow lawyers can be among the most supportive people in your life. Your decision to leave the career they chose can be challenging for them and for your relationship with them as well.

The first thing to clarify is whether the people you are worried about are actually going to react as negatively as you expect them to. Is it a fear or a fact? You may think that your relatives are going to be critical of your career change, but in fact they might find it an enormous relief to know that you are doing something that is likely to make you happier overall.

If people do react critically to your career change, it may help to understand where that criticism is coming from. There are at least four possibilities: (1) discomfort with something that doesn't conform to traditional narratives of success, (2) fear for your well-being, (3) jealousy of your courage, or (4) personal insecurity about their own career choices.

It's important to remember that negative reactions are often an awkward form of caring. For the most part, when concern comes from people who care about you, it is usually because those people want the best for you. The first reason, discomfort with deviation from the norm, comes from the natural human reaction against anything that we perceive as a threat. Our primal fight or flight responses don't just apply to predators in the woods. We are creatures driven to conformity partly because of our culture, including the influence of social media, and partly because of our natural instincts to stay close to the safety of the tribe.

The second reason is closely related to the first. Our protective instincts also kick in when a vulnerable member of the tribe steps outside the pack's protection. When someone goes off on a non-traditional exploration, the people who care for them may worry that the explorer won't be able to take care of herself. And the explorer herself may worry about that, too. How are you going to support yourself if you don't have a nice, stable law firm job? Many of these critics may be unaware of the high rate of turnover among law firm associates, the pyramidal framework of law firm structures that eliminate some associates by necessity as time goes on, or the increasing fluidity of career paths in general now. Or it may be that this concern is coming from parents who helped pay for law school with the understanding that the resulting JD would guarantee you a substantial and secure income that you now appear to be throwing out the window.

To the people who care about you, your most reassuring response may look something like this: "I appreciate your concern, and I know that you are only telling me this because you care about me. A lot of lawyers explore other options and become much happier as a result. I have a plan and a community of people who have done exactly this kind of exploring to support me. I'll be so grateful for your support as well."

The third and fourth reasons, jealousy and personal insecurity, are also related to each other. These are often the reactions of other lawyers, especially co-workers. Anyone who has accepted a career path because of its financial stability or because jobs in that field are easy to find may feel a jolt of surprise when someone else steps off a predictable career path in search of greater personal satisfaction. At some level, they may wonder whether they should have, or could do, the same thing. It won't surprise you to learn that jealous people are often unable to admit to or even recognize their own jealousy.

Reactions stemming from insecurity often take the form of a veiled (or not so veiled) insult. There may be a suggestion that you couldn't cut it as a lawyer, or that you weren't smart enough to succeed in a traditional legal career. You may sense that people think you are following a pipe dream or being irresponsible in some fundamental way that meets with their disapproval. If so, you are in excellent company: nearly every innovator and entrepreneur has encountered this kind of resistance from someone in their life along the way.

Responding to people whose root reactions come from some level of personal discomfort with what your decision implies about their decisions requires confidence and restraint. Remember, their reaction is about themselves, not a signal that you are actually on the wrong path. You don't need anyone else's seal of approval. It's wonderful to have their acceptance and support, of course, but the only person whose permission you truly need is your own.

Losing Your Identity and Finding It Again

Behind the fear of negative reactions and lost income is often something that is harder to articulate and confront: the loss of personal identity as a member of the legal profession. One of the first questions we ask each other in social situations is, "What do you do for a living?" Even for the unhappiest of lawyers, the ability to say, "I'm a lawyer" and to claim an affiliation with a firm can be reassuring. But what would you do if you no longer knew how to answer that question? The loss of identity that lawyers face when considering a career change can be profound.

For lawyers, this problem is especially pernicious because of the discrepancies between the promises the legal profession offers and the reality of law practice. The way the legal profession looks on TV and in the movies rarely matches the actual life of a lawyer, no matter what that lawyer does. As a college professor, Liz talks with a lot of undergraduate students who are thinking about law school. She usually offers to meet with them to try to talk them out of going to law school, which they find surprising coming from an experienced lawyer (but perhaps you don't). If she can talk them out of going to law school, she will have saved them at least three years of their lives and potentially hundreds of thousands of dollars. If she can't talk them out of going to law school, then they probably should go to law school after all.

The first question in every one of those conversations is this: Why do you want to go to law school? Many of the responses are similar to the ones we hear when we talk with unhappy lawyers. Liz also asks them the same question: If you can remember, why did you go to law school in the first place? The answers to this question often reveal a lot about why a lawyer is unhappy. Importantly, it can also provide critical information about the kind of career change that might be most satisfying for that lawyer now.

Take a moment and answer this for yourself: **Why did you go to law school in the first place?**

Here are some of the most common answers we have heard in working with unhappy lawyers.

1. I didn't know what else to do.

This is one of the most common responses we get when we ask people why they chose to get their Juris Doctor. Maybe you majored in History, or English, Literature, Social Studies, Philosophy, Government or a related field, and didn't see an obvious career path emerging from that degree. Academia might have been an option, but who wants to be in an ivory tower for the rest of their days? Law school can be an attractive option for liberal arts majors who want to increase their earning potential. It offers a somewhat stable, albeit decreasingly reliable, path to a secure job and an opportunity to earn a substantial starting salary after a relatively short time in graduate school. Compared with substantive doctorates, law school can be the path of least resistance for high-achieving and ambitious liberal arts graduates.

Law school has also been seen as a socially acceptable way to put off making a decision about your career. College students often hear that "you can do anything with a law degree." We agree with that statement, for the most part. The training law students receive and the skills they develop by practicing moot court, analyzing case law, and studying both the substance and procedure of law can be very useful in a wide range of careers. We will discuss that further throughout this book, especially in Chapters 7 and 8. Lawyers, given their training, can do just about anything, although some careers require more extensive formal retraining.

But it is also true that you can do anything without a law degree, except, of course, practice law. That is why it is so important for college students contemplating law school to understand precisely why they want to go to law school, and more specifically what kinds of law they most want to practice. Otherwise, law school is a very expensive way to spend three busy years deferring an important decision about what kind of career to pursue.

2. I'm good at arguing.

For some reason, many parents have been telling their argumentative children for decades that they should go to law school.

The problem this rationale often leads to is that arguing is only a small part of what lawyers do in general. Many lawyers don't engage in adversarial practice at all. Even litigators, the essence of whose work is advocating for one side or the other in a court case and preparing for such advocacy, spend a small part of their time actually arguing. And in bigger firms, lawyers spend even less time arguing in the traditional sense. We have worked with many Big Law associates who thought that they would spend more time in court than they do. Amy recalls the day she gave notice at her first law firm, a mid-size boutique law firm specializing in railroad and insurance defense litigation. When she told her supervising partner she was leaving to go to the litigation department at Skadden, he forecasted, "You'll hate it there. You're a litigator at heart and you will do very little actual litigation at a place like Skadden." Says Amy, "Within a year, I had to admit he was right."

Instead of arguing, litigation associates, particularly at big law firms, often find themselves in conference rooms, sorting through thousands and thousands of pages of e-files, or looking at box after box of paper documents. Instead of crafting clever arguments, these associates are more likely to be doing research into relevant case law and drafting memoranda about the holdings in various potentially relevant cases. Litigators even in the largest law firms can spend years between actual trials, since a high percentage of cases settle out of court. When they do argue motions, those motions are just as likely to concern dry issues of civil procedure as to encompass the kind of equity issues that people actually enjoy arguing about.

Many litigation associates find that the easiest route to the inside of a courtroom, and to the experience of arguing in court, is through representing clients *pro bono* in specialized court hearings. These might include appearing in family court, in housing court, or in eviction or bankruptcy proceedings. Those can be powerfully rewarding experiences for both the lawyer and the client. But for lawyers who take on *pro bono* clients, the cases are often undervalued or ignored for purposes of annual evaluations and promotions. The experience of arguing in court is often exciting, but it is unusual for those arguments to take up the majority of a lawyer's professional time. Lawyers who went to law school because they were good at arguing are often disappointed by the way their careers diverge from that ideal.

3. I like reading and writing.

The love of books also draws a lot of people to the legal profession. Maybe you have always loved reading. If, like Liz, you are awful at anything having to do with numbers, business school probably did not seem like a promising option for graduate study. If you are averse to studying biology and/or seeing blood, medical school might also have sounded like a bad option. Law school, on the other hand, appeared to involve a lot of reading. It may also have appeared to involve a lot of talking about the reading, like a very expensive book club. You may also have understood law school and/or the practice of law to require you to do a lot of writing. Lawyers write briefs and motions and memoranda all the time. From a distance, law school might look like a comfortable way for someone who loves reading and writing to spend a few years, and then to make tons of money after graduation. If you went to law school at least in part because you like reading and writing, you were bound to be disappointed.

Reading, both in law school and in law practice, bears no resemblance at all to the kind of reading most readers do for fun. Cases are constructed from rules and facts, written by judges who have no incentive to make their rulings easy or pleasant to read. In fact, when a decision includes language that is especially witty or enjoyable, lawyers celebrate that fact like a comet. For the most part, what we read as lawyers is functional, not fun. It is somewhat akin to drinking Gatorade instead of wine, except without the fun sports part preceding the Gatorade.

Writing, as a lawyer writes, is no better. Both of us love to write, but you may have noticed that we are no longer lawyers. That is in part because the kind of writing that lawyers do tends to deaden the soul, especially for creative types. It can be disappointing to learn that the only kind of writing lawyers are expected to do is analytical rather than literary. An associate tasked with drafting a memorandum about relevant case law probably will find herself penalized for any kind of literary flair she may bring to the exercise. Motions and briefs, of course, are governed by rules of civil procedure rather than rules of style. Many would-be writers go to law school because they think they will be able to write as part of their jobs, but the format of the writing required of lawyers can break their hearts.

We think that one of the reasons that there are so many former lawyers who write books is exactly because of this false promise. Lawyers who write romance novels, lawyers who write murder mysteries, and lawyers who just write are some of the happier lawyers we know. As Amy notes, "When I was a lawyer, I was a professional writer. But I left the law to find my own writing voice."

4. I want to pursue justice.

"Justice, justice, you shall pursue," says the Torah in the Book of Deuteronomy. Law is one of the few careers that offers both the potential to promote social justice through lasting change and some measure of financial security. The typically blindfolded figure of Justice is practically our mascot. The division of the federal government that actively practices law is the Department of Justice. In practice, however, the lawyers who do the most to promote justice are often some of the lowest paid members of the profession.

Many of the lawyers who are now in the later years of their practice started law school in the 1960s and 1970s, a time when idealism was particularly powerful in the United States. The influence of lawyers like Thurgood Marshall suggested that the practice of law might provide a way for people to create real and meaningful changes in society. Atticus Finch, the protagonist of Harper Lee's *To Kill a Mockingbird*, inspired many people who grew up loving that novel to go to law school in the 1970s and 1980s. Gloria Cordes Larson, the former President of Bentley University, recalled Atticus Finch as a singular influence and the main reason she went to law school after college, even though very few women around her were making the same choice. In the same era, Ruth Bader Ginsburg began to inspire people to enter the legal profession in much the same way, and she remains an inspirational figure for many lawyers and law students.

The ideals of law students who hope to pursue justice are often crushed by the reality of which kinds of companies can afford large law firms to represent them. The American Civil Liberties Union, the Southern Poverty Law Center and other progressive legal organizations are overwhelmed with applications for entry level positions that offer relatively low salaries, yet are immensely competitive. Private law firms, on the other hand, tend to offer very few opportunities to promote the public good. While the American Bar Association recommends that law firms offer *pro bono* opportunities, firms generally cap the percentage of an associate's billable hours requirement that can constitute *pro bono* work. Associates who do that work may find it personally rewarding but not necessarily valued as highly in their annual evaluations as service provided to paying clients of the firm.

Lawyers who do serve the public interest often find themselves burned out by the combination of high case load, low pay, and the intense, often life or death nature of the work itself. Public defenders are one example of lawyers who dedicate their time to protecting the rights of people accused of crimes, people who are often from underserved populations. This is critically important work, but it is not compensated accordingly. On the other side of the aisle, assistant attorneys general also complain of relatively low compensation for the work they do defending the interests of the state. On the other hand, lawyers who work in attorney generals' offices tend to experience higher levels of career satisfaction than lawyers in other kinds of practice.

5. Law looked like fun.

If you went to law school because you identified with the lawyers on a TV show, you are not alone. First, there was *L.A. Law*; then, *Ally McBeal*. More recently, shows like *Suits*, *Damages*, *The Good Wife*, and *How to Get Away With Murder* have depicted lawyers as glamorous figures who can easily afford gorgeous clothes, cars, and condominiums. If your only knowledge of the legal profession came from watching these shows, you would think that lawyers spend most of their time in beautiful conference rooms and court-rooms, spouting clever arguments and key facts without any preparation at all. Lawyers in the movies, especially from the 1990s onward, look much the same. Most young people don't know any lawyers personally, although they have almost all met doctors at some point in their lives. Without the counterbalance of real-life role models, it is understandable that these idealized images of lawyers would have a significant impact.

As any practicing lawyer will tell you, however, the reality of law practice looks nothing like what you see on TV. Every feat of verbal acrobatics and every persuasive argument, whether in a conference room or a courtroom, requires hours and hours of preparation, often on the backs of junior associates who may not even make it into the room. The billable hours required of law firm associates don't leave much time for shopping for those beautiful clothes and cars. The cases that settle, the failure to find case law on your side, the motions that are denied, the partners who ignore your work or ask for complex analyses on a Friday afternoon that are due on Monday morning, and the verdicts that are lost: none of those scenarios make it onto the screen. And yet, those realities are far more common than the images of lawyers most people see on television.

6. I wanted to make a lot of money.
Look, we get it. In the Fall of 2021, starting salaries for associates in New York law firms easily exceeded $200,000 per year. Few other professions offer the chance to make so much money after so little time in graduate school. That is especially true for people who are more literate than numerate.

But the promise of money often leads to unhappiness for lawyers in several ways. First, those starting associate salaries only go to the small fraction of law school graduates who win those positions. More often than not, those associates have graduated from some of the most prestigious law schools in the country. The majority of law school graduates do not go to those law schools and do not get those jobs. And even for those who do get those positions, the pyramidal nature of law firm structures means that those associates will get winnowed out, year by year. Over time, a small percentage of those associates will be promoted to partnership. The rest will move on: to other firms, to in-house positions, and out of law altogether. But most law firms do not prepare associates for those alternatives to promotion.

Second, money doesn't always buy happiness. It definitely buys prestige cars, houses, and luxury vacations. It provides undeniable security, as long as your expenses don't exceed that income. But if you are looking for a sense of self-worth, of accomplishment, or of contribution to something greater than yourself, money is a poor substitute. We do not mean to suggest that high salaries and societal contributions are mutually exclusive. They are not. But over time, the power of financial incentives can wane for people who are not being fulfilled in ways that are truly important to them.

As you can see, there are a lot of reasons that people go to law school and yet find themselves disappointed by the reality of law practice. There are as many subtleties to these scenarios as there are unhappy lawyers (that is to say, millions of them). Understanding the disconnects between the hopes you had when you entered law school and the realities of law practice can help you understand that **there is nothing wrong with you if you want to leave the law.** It is entirely normal to question your career choice, especially in a career that demands so much and bears so little resemblance to the idealized, highly paid, socially progressive, and glamorous ideas people have of lawyers from the outside.

Law firms, it should be said, don't encourage this kind of introspective thinking about whether the practice of law is, or remains, right for you. As we discuss more in Chapters 7 and 8, the skills lawyers develop in law school and in practice lend themselves to many different kinds of career success. The culture of law firms, especially Big Law, doesn't advertise that fact. Relatively few law firms offer help evaluating other career options for their employees. And even if they did, the time pressure that lawyers in private practice face leaves little time for introspection. Vague feelings of unhappiness tend to be swallowed down along with our lattes. We have depositions to prepare for, contracts to draft, and research to do. Every tenth of an hour we spend on personal matters is a tenth of a billable hour we have to make up somewhere else in the day.

What Do You Want to Have Done?

"I don't want to get to the end of my life and find that I have just lived the length of it. I want to have lived the width of it as well."
–Diane Ackerman

One of the most time-efficient and powerful exercises you can do to regain a sense of perspective is the Obituary Exercise. This asks you to take a stab at writing your own obituary, as you would like it to read, assuming that you have many years left to live. What do you want your obituary to be able to record about what you did with your life? It sounds morbid, and we felt a little creepy when we did it ourselves. That said, we strongly recommend doing this exercise before making a major career decision.

The purpose of the "write your own obituary" exercise is to reflect on the kind of life you want to lead by contemplating it in full. Most people do not think about their legacy, or the impact of their life, until they approach the end of it, by which time it is usually too late to make major changes. By doing this creative writing exercise, you give yourself the gift of time to adopt the changes you think you will be most proud of in your later years.

By stepping back to consider how you would like to be remembered, writing your own obituary gives you a rare opportunity to think about how your life is going while you still have time to redirect it. It can provide you with a new way to evaluate how you are spending your days, months, and years without imposing any other values but your own.

Writing your own obituary can also be a powerful tool for reflecting on your life as it is now. Describing your life in this way can reveal the extent to which you are happy with where you currently are and the choices you have made so far. If you were to die tomorrow, would you be happy with the legacy you leave behind? Have you made the kind of impact you wanted to make, whether on your family, friends, community or the world in general? What would people say about you and how you have lived your life so far?

This may sound hard at first. Who wants to confront their own mortality? Actually, most people who do this obituary exercise feel that way at first, and ultimately find it liberating and empowering. You may find that you are right on track in terms of living according to your own values and goals. Or you may find that you have been chasing something that won't matter as much in the long term, and that is not how you want to live your one precious life. The key is to figure out what adjustments you want to make while you still have time to make them.

The first step in this process is to familiarize yourself with obituaries, assuming you do not read them habitually. They usually capture basic information about where and when a person was born, the highlights of their education and career, the touchstones of their family life, and their notable achievements. Obituaries should not cover every event in a person's life, just the highlights as the writer defines them. In addition, obituaries often capture how the person will be remembered by those they leave behind. Although it may seem morbid to read the obituaries of strangers, it can be enlightening. Rather than looking them up online, you might also find brief obituaries of fellow graduates of your college or law school in your alumni magazine.

Next, think about a summary of how you would want to be remembered. What did you contribute? How did you help make the world a better place? Then outline what you are most proud of having done in your life. This might include personal accomplishments as well as professional milestones. Maybe you traveled to Machu Picchu or learned to play the ukulele. Maybe you were a proud Girl Scout Troop Leader, or amassed a phenomenal collection of Furbies. Anything that you're proud of should go on the list.

Consider, too, how people thought of you in terms of your personal qualities. What do you want people to remember most about you when you are gone? Perhaps you want to be thought of as kind and loving, or as a creative thinker. Maybe you hope to be remembered as the kind of person who connects others and has a wide network of friends.

The obituary exercise is most useful when you can't decide between two potential career paths. If you are not sure which path to take, write two alternative obituaries, one following your first option and a second following the other option. Which makes you feel more satisfied? More proud? Which is the life you would prefer to have lived? For example, let's say that you are a mid-level associate at a large law firm, and you are wondering whether to change careers to something more creative, like becoming a marketing director.

Begin by writing the obituary you could expect if you continued on the same path you are on now, without leaving the firm voluntarily. What do you think your life might look like overall, at the end of your career? What will you have accomplished professionally? What will you have accomplished in the areas or on the issues you care about personally? What kinds of relationships will you leave behind?

As you start writing this first obituary, you may start considering how important your current professional goals will seem to you at the end of your life. If you win that big case on behalf of a major tech company, what kind of an impact will that make in your life in 5, 10, or 30 years? What might you have to sacrifice in order to reach those goals? When you look back on what you have done with your time on earth—at least for the purposes of this exercise— how important will the promotions and raises you may have received be to you?

Next, write the second obituary. This is the one you might expect to have if you take the second path, leaving law to become a marketing director. There may be some gap months or years while you make that transition. But when you have started that next career, and followed that for some time, what difference might that make to your overall satisfaction with the life you have led? Would you have had more time to pursue the things you loved? Would you have been better able to form the kinds of friendships and family bonds that contribute to a life well lived? How, in fact, do **you** define a life well lived? The "write your own obituary" exercise may be the single best way to answer that question.

As you write, pay attention to how you choose what to highlight. Would you be most proud of achieving a certain title? Earning a particular salary? Enjoying a hobby or traveling to certain places? For Liz, writing her own obituary was one of the things that motivated her to write her first book. It was a life goal that she became more determined to complete once she reminded herself that she did not have an infinite amount of time to do so.

You may also find that this exercise reshuffles some of your priorities and reconnects you with the things that matter most. Creating at least one possible obituary for yourself helps you check in with yourself about the extent to which you are living in accordance with your values. It can illuminate not only what you want to change about your life, but the roles, relationships, and accomplishments of which you are already most proud.

As you draft your obituary, you will almost certainly confront the importance of personal connections. It can be easy to lose sight of the personal relationships in our lives and the strengths of our interpersonal bonds, especially when we are facing challenges at work. But what outlives us is the memories people have of us. For most people, those personal qualities and relationships will matter even more than our accomplishments to those we leave behind.

This is also an opportunity to rewrite how you want the rest of your life to go. If there is something you've always wanted to do but have been putting off, this may spur you to get it done. That could be getting more involved with a specific cause, traveling more intentionally, learning a new language, or taking on another project that has personal meaning to you. Including it in your obituary may strengthen your commitment to making it a reality.

For our purposes, the most important benefit of writing your own obituary is that it helps you determine what the right path forward is, given your values and goals. There are no wrong answers to these questions. The only wrong way to make career decisions is not to examine them at all.

CHAPTER 5

The Goldilocks Method of Leaving: How to Avoid Leaving Too Soon or Too Late

"I breathe differently."[70]
—Shunta Grant, lawyer turned entrepreneur and business coach

The Quest for Just Right

IF YOU WERE IN LAW SCHOOL in the mid-1990s (like we were!) your torts classes likely talked passionately about the "hot coffee" lawsuit against McDonald's that was unfolding in real time. Believed at the time to be a frivolous lawsuit in which a claimant was, somewhat incredibly, awarded nearly $3 million for being served coffee that was hot, the case of *Liebeck v. McDonald's* became an interesting discussion piece for proving the essential elements of a tort case. Ultimately, the case turned on damning documents, testimony, and corporate greed for refusing to settle for the initial $20,000 demand for medical bills.[71] It turned out coffee really could be "too hot."

Perhaps buoyed by the McDonald's "too hot" result, claimants nearly two decades later attempted to bring some "too cold" lawsuits against Starbucks, alleging Starbucks loaded their drinks with too much ice. These lawsuits were met with less favorable results (from the plaintiffs' perspectives).[72] It turned out, then, that coffee could really be "just right."

Is the same true about leaving the law? Is there ever a "just right" time to leave the law? We believe there is. And not surprisingly, it's the time that falls exactly between leaving too soon and too late. And if you're thinking there's got to be more to it than that: well done, Counselor. Here's how to map out your own timeline.

Don't Leave Now: the Argument Against Leaving TOO SOON

It's generally a bad idea to run out the door at the lowest point of your legal career. If that moment feels like now, and if you have a choice, it's much better to plan out your pre-flight checklist[73], growing your money and connections (including the goodwill of junior colleagues, which is a sometimes ignored commodity on the way out the door of any career). These and more will be necessary for the next leg of the journey as you transition away from the practice of law.

Of course, the pre-flight time is about more than networking and saving. It's also about cultivating wellness and healthy attitudes that will propel you in the next chapter. Importantly, you need to accept that it's not "too soon" to leave just because you don't know exactly what to do next.

Many transitioning lawyers describe that period of time before they left the practice of law as the time that they still didn't know what they didn't know, so "over-planning" the next steps isn't helpful, possible, or even productive. The pre-flight checklist is about readying yourself for the next steps but it doesn't necessarily mean you know exactly what the next steps look like.

Take for example, Kat Johnson, a former high-powered Silicon Valley attorney who says she used the length of time she'd been in the practice and the clout she'd cultivated, to work on drawing some boundaries for herself and working on wellness goals without running out the door at the moment of burnout.[74] She ultimately transitioned to become a wellness retreat coordinator, after a self-described two-year "plan-less" period of time.

Of course, achieving wellness goals and carving out time for reflection so that she could be open to a new career path outside the practice of law was an important step for her. It was her way of overcoming the inertia that many would-be transitioning attorneys get stuck at: that 'but-where-do-I-start" stumbling block.[75] Says Johnson, "Ultimately I had to let go of the idea that I need to know what's next before I leave this career."[76]

Is It Time to Leave Yet?

A common challenge unhappy lawyers face is how to tell the difference between garden variety job dissatisfaction and something more significant. On her blog, The Unbillable Life, Marissa Geannette offers advice to people who are trying to decide when it is time to leave Big Law.[77] She offers a list of signs that it might be time to quit, including the following:

1. Feeling jealous of everyone else whose job looks less demanding or stressful than yours.

2. Developing health problems and/or the inability to make time to take care of your health.

3. Overwhelming feelings of anxiety when you think about going back to the office on Monday (although in our experience it is common for Big Lawyers to work through the weekend anyway).

4. Failing to take vacations in which you actually disconnect from work, or to show up for the major life events of your friends.

To this list we would add "reading a book called *How to Leave the Law.*" There are so many indicators that something needs to change that it would be impossible to list them all. Your own gut instinct, which may be hard to listen to at first, is the best indicator that you should at least investigate and compare some other options.

Ideally you'll do work both internally and externally before your transition to make it as seamless as possible. You'll acknowledge the challenges you might face without accepting them as defeat. You will address head on the likely identity struggle, as you begin the process of reframing and redefining what it means to "be a lawyer" as discussed in Chapter 4.

And yes, part of cultivating a wellness strategy will include a hard look at money. The financial cost of transitioning in any professional journey cannot and should not be ignored. Life coach and author of *Thoughtfully Fit*, Darcy Luoma, in describing her own transition from education/politics to life coaching has talked about the importance of getting the financial pieces in place so one doesn't have to operate from a "place of fear."[78] Of course it's impossible to remove fear completely from the equation of a transition. But it is possible to minimize the chance that fear drives your decision-making.

Developing Risk Tolerance

One of the most important and most difficult parts of leaving the law is getting comfortable with the risk involved in any change. Risk is especially challenging for lawyers to confront. We are, in general, a risk-averse group of people. Many lawyers devote their professional lives to mitigating risk, whether by carefully drafting contract provisions that anticipate and resolve potential conflicts, or by identifying potential risks in business practices that could lead, or have led, to litigation. Many lawyers are, to put it plainly, paid to worry for other people. Asking lawyers to take on risks in their own lives can cause a temporary short circuiting in the brain. It is contrary to our nature, at least as a group of professionals.

But all change involves risk. Contemplating any kind of professional transition requires accepting some amount of discomfort. The same is true for any other major life decision, like having a child or buying a house. What if it doesn't go well? What if I regret my decision? The fear can be paralyzing.

Becoming more comfortable with risk is a gradual process. And in this context, it is one you can manage at your own pace. Unlike many major life decisions, however, there are ways to minimize the risk of the unknown when you are making a career change. You can, for example, build up your career risk tolerance over time, by making small changes. In our experience, listening to your intuition in making decisions generally leads to making better decisions over time.

Getting more comfortable making decisions is closely related to getting comfortable with risk. It is perhaps surprisingly easy to go through life without ever making a hard decision. From high school to college, we are usually given narrow parameters about any decision we have to make. Choosing a college is a matter of where you get in. That, in turn, is a function of where you have applied, which depended on where you were likely to get in based on your grades, test scores, and demographic profile. The classes you took in college and law school were limited by institutional constraints like the numbers of credits you needed, or the classes that were available to you in any given semester. For many lawyers, even choosing law school wasn't much of a choice at all. If you were good at writing, arguing, or logic puzzles, law school might have been the most appealing of the usual post-graduate options.

If you are reading this book, you have already had the experience of making a choice about law school and/or about your legal career that you either doubt or regret. So it is no wonder that when it comes to changing careers, many lawyers freeze up at the idea of making the wrong choice. Most of us do not feel great about at least one major career-related decision we have made in the past.

And there are risks whether you decide to make a change or not. If you are worried about making the wrong decision about your career, think about the risks of staying in an unsatisfying career for the wrong reasons. There is no guarantee that any career will be the perfect solution for the rest of your working life, but there are options that are more likely to result in having a job that you actually like and that allow you to use your natural strengths most if not all of the time.

Making the best possible choice about your career, at the moment when you make it, does not guarantee that your choice will be perfect, then or forever. It does not mean that your career is going to turn out the way you want it to and that you are going to be happy for the rest of your life with your choice. Even the most fulfilled people will tell you that there are parts of their ideal jobs that are not ideal. Liz, for example, loves being a professor except for the part of the job where she has to grade her students at the end of the term. Amy loves writing but finds the marketing part of her job as novelist very time-consuming and cuts into the time she actually gets to write. But if you make that decision carefully and methodically, using expert guidance and your own introspective wisdom, you minimize the risk that you will make a choice that you come to regret.

Put simply, addressing risk is the most important step in the pre-flight checklist. You'll never remove all of the risk or fear from your transition from law, but you're a lawyer. You can certainly work toward minimizing the risk to an acceptable or more comfortable level. And the best way to do this is to make sure you don't leave too soon.

To avoid leaving too soon and thereby minimize risks involved in transitioning, consider these four steps: acknowledge the culture of unwellness and assess the viability of reversing the culture in your particular circumstance; regain control/autonomy; improve your capacity for resilience; and change your relationship with your law firm salary (save it, stop hoarding it, stop disposing of it, and most importantly, stop relying on it). Finally, note these four steps should really be employed at the same time, rather than seriatim.

Assess the Viability of Reversing the Culture of Unwellness in Your Circumstance

A crucial step in reversing the culture of unwellness in your particular situation is to denounce the stigma associated with challenging the culture and acknowledging resulting disorders including depression, mental health challenges, and prevalent substance abuse. The first step can be simply starting a dialogue with someone.

The 2017 Report of the National Task Force on Lawyer Well-Being ("2017 Report on Lawyer Well-Being"), which was drafted by a collection of entities within and outside the ABA, makes a number of recommendations to help combat the culture of unwellness in contemporary legal practice, including to facilitate, destigmatize, and encourage help-seeking behaviors.

The 2017 Report on Lawyer Well-Being states that "[r]esearch shows that the most effective way to reduce stigma is through direct contact with someone who has personally experienced a relevant disorder. Ideally, this person should be a practicing lawyer or law student (depending on the audience)."[79] To that end, the Task Force Report notes that:

> The military's "Real Warrior[s]" mental health campaign can serve as one model for the legal profession. It is designed to improve soldiers' education about mental health disorders, reduce stigma, and encourage help seeking. Because many soldiers (like many lawyers) perceive seeking help as a weakness, the campaign also has sought to re-frame help-seeking as a sign of strength that is important to resilience. It highlights cultural values that align with seeking psychological help."[80]

In fact, we believe the Real Warriors campaign is more than just a general inspirational model. It has concrete application in the world of the would-be transitioning lawyer. In addition to seeking out dialogue with current and transitioning lawyers, here are several tools used in the Real Warriors campaign that we would recommend employing as you work to reverse the culture of unwellness in your own circumstance:

- **Positive use of social media.**[81] To this end, social media can be used to identify and communicate with transitioning lawyers in a wide range of "after law" professional fields. Social media can also be used to maintain (or in some instances, regenerate) social relationships that are difficult to nurture alongside the demands of a legal practice. The strength of your social network (both with lawyers and non-lawyers) will help you prepare for a big life transition like leaving the law.

- **Navigate change through writing.**[82] According to the Real Warriors Campaign, writing helps with stress and focus, as it can center the mind, reduce negative, hopeless thoughts, and help generate and focus on solutions. These same benefits can apply to a would-be legal transitioner as well.

- **Spend time translating your past experience by looking closely at your technical skills, interpersonal skills, and leadership skills.**[83] Once you do this, you can work on ways to communicate them without legal jargon or legalese (e.g., legal briefs and e-discovery are now research, writing, and categorizing large sets of complicated data points).

Regain Control/Autonomy

As you work to reverse the culture of unwellness, and employ wellness techniques that will serve you in your next chapter, you will want to also be proactive in your choices and movement forward. You want to avoid leaving as a reaction. Instead you want to be in control of your exit, and a good way to ensure this is to regain control/autonomy of your career itself. Or perhaps, regain is not the appropriate term if you've been on autopilot for much of your professional journey. This is your time to "gain" control once and for all.

Too many of us fall victim to the ideology that the incentives and perks of a legal career are themselves the reward. But if that were true, the big paychecks of Big Law careers would be enough to make any and all Big Law attorneys happy. Of course, the rates of depression and anxiety in law and Big Law in particular belie that conclusion. What then is missing in a career where the pay and power is high but the job satisfaction is low?

Consider this study[84] which looked at 2,000 students, to determine whether their growth mindset (that is, the understanding that their abilities and understanding could be developed according to hard work) was affected by incentives that both did and did not undermine their autonomy. In looking at various incentives for hard work, the researchers found that without a sense of autonomy, incentives actually undermined the performance of those participants who had high initial achievement.[85]

Is there, then, a way for you to shift your mindset in your own practice in a way that not only gathers up perks and incentives, but also improves autonomy? One of the most significant ways to do so is to remove barriers between yourself and the end product, a significant problem in Big Law. In our interviews with lawyers, it seems consistently true that those closest to the client in the chain of service have the most job satisfaction and longevity. And yet, solo and small firm practice simply isn't supported or encouraged at the law school model. Starting your own firm or working for a smaller firm is generally thought to be the outcome for those who don't get a top-tier law firm gig first. What if we reject this model and cultivate a legal practice that puts you close to the client and close to the end product? In the Big Law environment, a viable way to achieve this is by taking on a *pro bono* matter for your department. Does this level of autonomy incentivize you more than law firm car service and expense accounts? Does it change your attitude toward the practice of law? Does that reverse the burnout you feel?

The 2017 Report on Lawyer Well-Being addresses head on the difference between work engagement and burnout. When resources (i.e., positive individual, job, and organizational factors, like autonomy, good leadership, supportive colleagues, feedback, interesting work, optimism, resilience) outweigh demands (i.e., draining aspects of the job, like work overload and conflicting demands) then engagement occurs. When demands overtake the equilibrium, then burnout occurs. Ask yourself whether you can make a shift back to the place where resources outweigh demands, before leaving the practice altogether, or even your current position. In this way, you can avoid leaving too soon.

Improve Your Capacity for Resiliency

If you're well into your pre-flight checklist, and you're still convinced that taking a break from the law is right for you, be sure to cultivate some resiliency first. But is resiliency something that can, in fact, be cultivated? Is resilience innate or is it the product solely of our upbringing and childhood experiences? Well, the short answer is "both," but there's even more to it than that.

Dr. Karen Reivich, researcher and Author of *The Resilience Factor*, admits that in undertaking resiliency study, her bias was that resilience was something we were hard wired for, and you have it or you don't. But she was proven wrong. Resilience, it seems, can be taught. Dr. Reivich is the Director of Training Programs at the University of Pennsylvania Positive Psychology Center. She is an internationally recognized expert in the fields of resilience, depression prevention, and Positive Psychology. She has more than 30 years of experience developing and delivering resilience and Positive Psychology programs for educators and their students, U.S. Army soldiers, health care professionals, a professional sports organization, corporate audiences, and more. As lead instructor of the Penn Resilience Program, she has worked with more than 10,000 participants.

While she characterizes herself as naturally leaning toward negativity and pessimism, Dr. Reisich's conclusion is overwhelmingly positive, as she notes: "Resilience is under your control. You can teach yourself to be resilient. You can profoundly change how well you handle setbacks, how enthusiastically you approach challenges."[86]

Neurobiologists have actually found that we can retrain our brains when we redirect negative thoughts. What are some ways to cultivate resilience while still practicing law? What if you stopped talking about hating your job, your office, and the practice of law itself? What if instead you retrain your thoughts to verbalize daily the aspects you like best about the practice? You can then cultivate a list of transferable skills while simultaneously growing your capacity for resiliency.

You can also retrain your thoughts about transitioning from the law from catastrophizing to positive leaning. Goli Kalkhoran, founder of *Lessons of A Quitter*, says one of the most important lessons she has learned in the years since she left the law is that it's important to counter the thought "what if the worst happens" with "but what if it turns out even better than you could imagine?"[87]

In sum, research and neurobiology shows that resiliency can be honed like a muscle with positive thinking and an active gratitude practice, preferably daily. The 2017 Report on Lawyer Well-Being recommends improving the capacity for resiliency through "optimism, confidence in our abilities and strengths (self-efficacy), effective problem solving, a sense of meaning and purpose, flexible thinking, impulse control, empathy, close relationships and social support, and faith/spirituality."[88]

Of course, there are nuances to making the argument that resiliency and other competencies can be learned and taught. And it's important that the ability to control and cultivate resiliency should not be used as a weapon against those who choose to leave the legal arena rather than withstand it.[89]

In their article, authors Nikolai Münch, Hamideh Mahdiani, Klaus Lieb, and Norbert W. Paul point out: "Understanding resilience as a kind of personal empowerment is made possible by delegating the responsibility to foresee and prevent negative psycho-cognitive impacts of lived experience to the individual herself. If resilience is something one can learn and train, then everybody can do something to survive (or even grow) in the face of adversity. This view gets especially problematic if resilience as a discourse is focused solely on the individual and is not complemented by considering social problems and dysfunctional social structures."[90]

Put simply, the fact that resiliency can be taught and learned and cultivated by the individual, should empower lawyers in various stages of their training and career; however, it does not mean that law firms and the legal profession can forfeit their responsibility for the conditions and disparities at play that might make it difficult and increasingly impossible for individuals to continue in the profession.

Change Your Relationship With Your Law Firm Salary

The financial considerations of a transition from the practice of law are important. But in addition to saving some predetermined amount of money before leaving after consideration of fixed and non-fixed expenses, you must go a step further. You have to fundamentally change your relationship with your law firm salary, and ultimately change your relationship with money.

Jessica Medina is a Columbia Law School grad and Big Law survivor, and also a veteran of the SEC. She is currently an Accredited Financial Counselor and works specifically with lawyers thinking about making a switch.[91] Medina employs what she calls "an intense Esquire Strategy Session" with her transitioning lawyer clients where she works closely with them in deep diving into their top financial questions including:

· Can I afford to leave my job?

· What happens if I move?

· How can I optimize my finances so that I can later
leave my job?

As Medina points out, lawyers are not necessarily trained in business or finance. "So many of us were never given basic personal finance education, or find that the typical advice just doesn't apply to us (hello average student loan debt of $145,000 for law school grads!) so I intend to fill that gap."

Medina recommends her clients take a hard look at expenses

including mortgage and child care and grade their debt. For example, some low interest loans (e.g., certain student loans) should not be paid off in a hurry. But one of the most important lessons Medina hopes to pass on to her transitioning lawyer clients is to reframe the money worth perspective that lawyers often internalize due to the billable hour model.

"It can be so damaging to tie your worth to money, especially when that money is tied to time. Shifting away from focusing on money as a measure of worth is no small task after working in a field defined by the billable hour." Medina says, "I ask my clients to think about what kind of life and work would make them truly happy. Often this involves some sort of service or higher good, and that work doesn't always pay Big Law money, but it pays for itself in fulfillment and overall happiness."

Of course, others caution not to get caught up in the notion that you can never make as much money as you did practicing law. Lessons From a Quitter Founder, Goli Kalkorhan says this was a myth she finally broke through in 2021, when she made six figures with her business/podcast by mid-year. The goal is to change your reliance on your salary so that you can make more informed decisions from a place of power, and not fear.

Hopefully, by now, we can agree that it's important to avoid leaving too soon. And yet, recognizing that perfection is difficult to achieve, the corollary to the Goldilocks Timeline is the Blackjack Timeline: i.e., come as close as you can to the right time, without going over.

Don't Leave Then: the Argument Against Leaving TOO LATE

Goli Kalkhoran describes the "Sunk Cost Fallacy" that keeps many would-be transitioning lawyers in the trenches too long. Many lawyers are convinced that given the money and time they've invested in their legal education and training, the investment would be "wasted" if they leave the law.[92] This mentality, of course, fails to recognize the versatility of the legal education and training and assumes the only natural outcome is climbing the rungs of a law firm. The stories of successful JDs in arenas including marketing, finance, education, creative fields, entrepreneurial ventures, and more, belie this assumption.

It's important when evaluating whether the time is just right to leave (or as close as possible), to evaluate whether continuing to invest your finances and your time will yield any additional experience, connection, and/or confidence that will help in the next step of your professional life, or whether continued investment, particularly in the area of *time*, will yield no demonstrable positive results. This evaluation will necessarily require a shift in the mental space that dictates the sunk cost fallacy. The time previously invested is not wasted.

Consider advice of former Wall Street Trader Bill Perkins, espoused in the Wall Street Journal Bestseller, *Die With Zero*. With advice endorsed by *Shark Tank's* Barbara Corcoran, and others, Perkins, opens *Die With Zero* with an ecdote about a successful lawyer who received a cancer diagnosis at 35, and died three months later. A startling and incredibly relevant answer to the question at hand here.

Interestingly, Perkins is not a financial planner. He's an engineer, and he says the question of when to stop doing the things we no longer want to do is an "optimization problem: how to maximize fulfillment while minimizing waste."[93]

Perkins boldly points out the extreme example of Bill Gates, well known philanthropist, who can't seem to donate his money faster than it grows. "At least Gates had the wisdom and foresight to stop working for money when he was still young enough to start spending it in a big way. Too many wealthy, successful people fail to do that. And even Gates should have retired from paying work sooner, before accumulating several times what he could spend in one lifetime ... [M]any people ... just keep earning and earning, trying to maximize their wealth without giving nearly as much thought to maximizing what they get out of that wealth, including what they can give to their children, their friends, and the larger society now, instead of waiting until they die."[94]

The takeaway, says Perkins, is that "[t]he utility of money declines with age."[95] Thus, spend it and use it now: on yourself, on your favorite charity, on your children. Because eventually we will be older and our health will be on the decline and we will wonder why we waited so long to actually *use* the money we are earning.

Far from advocating frivolous spending, Perkins recommends investing in your health and free time. Perkins says: "Outsource the chores that can get you more free time, and spend money on your health."[96] Perkins compellingly cites the research of Bronnie Ware, an Australian palliative caregiver who cited the number one regret of people on their deathbed: the wish that they'd had the courage to live a life true to themselves rather than the life others expected of them.

And their second most common regret? *I wish I hadn't worked so damn hard.*[97]

And One More R: Robin!

One could say that the Goldilocks method boils down to the Four R's: Risk, Resources, Resilience, and Resolve. But we would add in one more R to the mix: Robin.

The advice of Robin Arzon, formerly a lawyer, now an instructor and Vice President of Fitness Programming at the mega-fitness business, Peloton, has recounted how she was held as a hostage at gunpoint in a bar in New York City while she was in college.[98] The fear and trauma led her to find an outlet in fitness that she ultimately decided to merge with her professional career instead of keeping it separate. But more than that, she says, "Ever since that day, I've actually lived every day as my last."

The extreme nature of Arzon's trauma may not necessarily be relatable for all of us, but the lesson learned can be. If you've ever taken a class with Arzon on Peloton, you know she's prone to advising that time is our most precious resource, as it is strictly non-renewable.

It's important to find that sweet spot in your career when you're not running out the door, solely in reactive mode. Instead, take control of your professional future and regain your autonomy. Relearn your relationship with money, eliminate your reliance and your concept of worth on your Big Law salary, but understand that money can still be earned outside of the law. Understand that success can still be earned outside of the law. Cultivate your capacity for resilience by retraining your negative thinking and improving your social network.

And then look around and ask yourself, if you had to live your last day today ... would you want it to be inside your current law firm?

CHAPTER 6

What to Ask Before Leaving Your Firm

"While I loved the advocacy and relationship-building aspect of law,
I craved something more creative."[99]

—Julie Schechter, lawyer turned entrepreneur

WHEN YOU KNOW SOMETHING is wrong at work, how do you know
whether that means that you should leave your job or make a less
drastic change? If you are like most lawyers we know, you're hoping
for the latter. The great news is that it is much easier to fine tune
your legal career from inside a firm now than it was even ten or
fifteen years ago. In this chapter, we'll explore the many ways to
change some aspect of your legal career without actually leaving
the law.

The feeling of being uncomfortable as an associate is wildly
familiar to most people who have worked in a law firm. There are
so many aspects of legal practice that law school does not teach. It
is easy to feel overwhelmed as a junior associate, especially when
you are used to mastering your classes, as you may have done in
college and law school. Law firms often mark the end of formal
training, and firms vary a lot in terms of the quality and extent of
their onboarding and inhouse training. From the moment you
enter a law firm as an associate, nothing is familiar. For most
lawyers, the first weeks of law practice are their first exposure to a
full-time, white-collar job. Summer associate programs are notoriously unrealistic preparation for the actual practice of law.
Learning how to work with paralegals and assistants is at least as
challenging as learning how to work with more senior associates
and partners. And what counts as billable work may not always be

clear. Especially for type A people who are used to excelling at whatever they do, law firms can be daunting from the outset.

Even as a mid-level associate or as a junior partner, there are new aspects of practice to learn on the job, usually without formalized training. Lawyers learn from other lawyers, whether it is by emulating what someone else does well or, frequently, by avoiding the practices that we see as harmful. Liz learned how to manage other associates in part by identifying the mistakes her own supervisors made, and then doing the opposite. It was not optimal.

Does that discomfort mean that practicing law is not right for you? Not necessarily. There are several decision points to address before deciding that leaving the law is the right choice.

Question 1: Would you be happier if you got additional training in your own firm?

The first question to ask yourself is why you are uncomfortable. Pinpointing the source can help you determine whether your discomfort comes from not knowing how to do some aspect, or several aspects, of your job well. The practices of doing legal research, drafting motions, navigating procedural rules, preparing depositions and drafting contracts are all fundamentally different in practice than they are in class or clinics.

Many firms offer in-house training programs or structured mentoring to help associates develop these key skills. The problem is that many associates can't or won't ask for help. It is common for unhappy lawyers to keep their misery close to their chest until they finally sever ties with their firms. Junior associates often think that they should know how to do their job without additional training, often because senior lawyers suggest as much or say so directly. And while there used to be a widespread culture of self-sufficiency among associates, that is changing across the country. More and more firms are incorporating training in legal practice skills as a regular part of the support they offer to lawyers. Asking for more training, which might once have been seen as a sign of weakness, is now widely accepted and supported in law firms as a rule.

But maybe the problem is not confidence in your skills or the ability to do your job well. Maybe you just don't like your job, no matter how well you do it. If that is the case, you may be tempted to conclude that the problem lies with your particular firm. Maybe you haven't found a practice group or a team that you click with. Maybe the culture of the firm is not what you signed up for. At this point, you may start wondering whether you chose the right law firm, or whether the problem lies with law in general.

Question 2: Would you be happier if you went to a different law firm?

This is the point at which many lawyers start answering calls from recruiters. We would caution you to make this decision especially carefully. If you don't like practicing law at your firm, the problem is not always solved by going to another firm. This can be extremely disappointing because moving to another firm is usually the easiest fix. Large firms, in particular, experience so much turnover that it is not hard to move from one to another. Legal recruiters commonly cold call associates to ask if they are looking to make a change. If that call comes in soon after a partner has yelled at you or asked you at 6pm on Friday to draft a 30-page memo by Monday morning, that can be a tempting call to answer.

One of the complaints we hear most often is that lawyers are suffering from the people who mismanage them. Law firms are notoriously full of bad managers. Law schools do not teach managerial skills, and many law firms do not focus on training mid-level lawyers to be effective managers. In litigation departments, particularly, the adversarial skills that might make a trial lawyer stellar in the courtroom might make that same lawyer a nightmare as a supervisor. But law firms are not the only places with bad managers. If you are leaving your law firm because you don't like the people you work for, then, it is worth taking a closer look at whether leaving your firm is likely to result in the kind of increased happiness you are looking for.

If that's the reason you want to leave the law, it is also worth asking whether there is anything you can do to protect yourself from a bad boss, either at your law firm or elsewhere. Setting boundaries about when you respond to a 2am email from a senior partner, for example, may feel uncomfortable at first, but may not result in your being fired or passed over for a promotion. The expectation that associates will work around the clock even on assignments that are not time sensitive is not universal. If you feel obligated to respond to that 2am email by 3am, it might be worth asking your supervisor explicitly if that is actually what they expect. It may be that they work best in the middle of the night, but not that they need an answer from you right away. If your reasons for wanting to leave your law job have more to do with the nature of the work, then it makes much more sense to consider an alternative career, which we discuss more in Chapters 10 and 11.

Sometimes moving to another firm is the right choice, but more often than not, associates swap one set of problems for another. Switching firms is usually a good long-term fix only in certain limited cases. Perhaps Firm B has a significantly more generous family leave policy, mentoring structure, or off-ramping program than Firm A. Maybe Firm B has an entirely different practice area that you are fairly sure you want to focus on instead of what you have been doing at Firm A. If that is the case, it is important to make sure that your offer is to practice in that new area rather than just having it be one possible outcome of your move. Or maybe you want to live in another city, and Firm B is willing to offer you a place there but Firm A can't offer you either the chance to work in that city's office or to work remotely on a permanent basis.

In any of these situations, getting a guarantee of the change you're looking for before you accept the position is critical. Any time you switch jobs, you give something up. You lose something of the relationships you have built as well as the personal knowledge you have gained about working with individual team members. Starting over in a new environment is stressful and challenging, even when it is the right move. For that reason, it is worth taking the time to make sure you are getting the bargain you want in the process.

Question 3: Would you be happier if you went in-house?

One of the most common transitions for junior associates is to go in-house. Moving to a general counsel's office can look like the perfect transition: it eliminates billable hours, appears to give you a more flexible and humane work life, and takes you out of the competitive race toward partnership, a life that many associates don't actually want when they learn more about it. Most companies hire in-house counsel from law firms in order to get junior counsel who have already trained in practicing law.

Before you look for an in-house position, consider having a frank conversation about your goals with someone you trust. Most unhappy associates only let people at their law firm know that they are leaving when they are on their way out the door. To some degree, that is understandable. In many firms, there has been a culture of almost shaming people who leave for in-house positions. Some less enlightened senior lawyers may see leaving the firm as a sign of weakness, a lack of dedication, or an indication that the associate is not truly cut out for the practice of law. It can also be hard to tell a more senior attorney that you are opting out of her own career path. It can feel like you are delivering a personal rejection in addition to choosing another kind of job. But that is rarely the case.

Jennifer Rakstad, Senior Learning and Development Manager for the Americas at White & Case, advises unhappy lawyers to think about the law firm's perspective in dealing with this kind of situation.[100] The last thing any law firm wants is to sever a relationship with an associate they have nurtured and helped to train. Although many lawyers are afraid that they will stop getting work, or even get fired, if they speak up about their dissatisfaction, she has never seen that happen in her more than 15 years of associate career development work.

The smartest course of action for any unhappy lawyer is to find a trusted confidant, within the firm if at all possible. Jennifer recommends setting up a time to talk with an ally, mentor, sponsor or a trusted partner. Scheduling that time in advance is important because it gives you an opportunity to practice what you are going to say with a friend or peer first.

You may even be able to take advantage of the firm's career coach, if there is one, to practice this conversation. White & Case, for example, has a coaching office where associates can book a time to practice difficult conversations. In this conversation, focus on the positives. DO say things like, "I have learned so much from my time here" and "I see my career going in a different direction." DO NOT say things like "I can't see myself working as hard as you do" or "I don't want to have your lifestyle."

It may help to remember that it is in the firm's interest to maintain a strong relationship with you and help you find the right landing spot. That spot could be with a client as an in-house attorney or it could be within the firm in a different role. She recalls one associate who didn't explain why she was dissatisfied until she gave notice. Had she spoken up sooner, Jennifer observed, the firm could have found a different type of work or even a different role for her. The benefits of speaking up far outweigh the potential downsides.

Increasingly, law firms are finding new ways to support lawyers who want to leave the firm to go in-house. Several leading firms have developed entire support systems for this purpose, treating attorneys who have left the firm as alumni to be celebrated and showcased. Kirkland & Ellis, for example, offers a CareerLink service to its alumni, including confidential career coaching, networking assistance, and job postings exclusively for the benefit of its current and former attorneys. Kirkland refers to the participants in this program as "colleagues for life": a brilliant way for the firm to maintain connections with a broad range of professionals. It is, of course, in their interest to do so. Happy in-house counsel are more likely to hire Kirkland as outside counsel, and more likely to recommend Kirkland to other companies in their sector if they have a strong ongoing relationship. And unhappy lawyers are likely to leave anyway. Why not help them get jobs within Kirkland's existing client base, and keep them in the family?

There are several aspects of moving in-house that you should consider before taking the leap. First, there are various kinds of in-house roles, regardless of seniority. Some companies are looking for compliance lawyers. Other in-house counsel focus on human resources management or developing contracts. Some roles focus on managing outside counsel for the purposes of antitrust, intellectual property, or other kinds of litigation. Some companies hire in-house counsel who can do a little of all of these things. When considering an in-house role, make sure you understand exactly what the position involves, and how well that role matches your own skills and interests.

Being clear about the day-to-day responsibilities of an in-house job is as important as understanding its purpose within the company. Be sure that you understand what that role involves in practice. One senior associate who left her Los Angeles law firm to join one of the Big Four accounting firms was looking forward to her new role managing litigation. What she didn't anticipate was how much of her time she would spend sitting in on depositions all over the country. What initially seemed like a lower stress job ended up requiring less intellect and more travel than she expected, and she left the job after two years.

In-house positions all have one thing in common: they eliminate the billable hour requirement. In-house counsel generally have more control over their time, and therefore, have more control over their work-life balance, than outside counsel. Evenings and weekends are more likely to be your own. It is common for in-house counsel to start their days between 8 and 9am and to work until 5 or 6pm. The days, however, are packed with individual conversations and group meetings. There doesn't tend to be a lot of time for research and analysis.

Unlike outside counsel, in-house lawyers have to be quick on their feet much of the time. While outside counsel research options and then present them to the client, in-house lawyers are the client. They are often called on to decide whether a proposed plan involves an acceptable amount of legal risk. They also need to know when to escalate that decision to someone more senior. In-house counsel have to be more comfortable "living in the gray zone" rather than just advising someone else about the risks.

In-house work also differs from law firm work in the ways people are brought in and promoted. In most law firms, new classes of associates come in every year and there is a fair amount of turnover, especially at the more junior levels. If an associate doesn't get along with a particular partner, or prefers a different practice area, she can often work with a different partner without losing any ground within the firm overall. In-house counsel tend to work with the same group of people for many years. If an in-house lawyer doesn't get along with her supervisor, there are fewer options. And people tend to come and go less often in companies than they do in law firms. Rather than getting annual lockstep raises, as associates do, in-house counsel may be compensated and receive raises according to an entirely different system.

A major potential downside of moving in-house is that your role changes from rock star to naysayer. In law firms, the lawyers are the main attraction because the primary function of a law firm is to provide legal advice. In business, lawyers are not valued the same way. Instead of driving value, they are more often seen as impediments to getting things done. Of course, in-house counsel play a critical role in mitigating risk and making it possible for a company to go on achieving its own primary purpose, but most non-lawyers do not see them that way.

Before accepting an in-house offer, then, it's important to consider the following:

1. What will you be doing day to day? How do your responsibilities change over the course of the year?

2. What are your standard working hours? Under what circumstances would you need to work evenings and/or weekends, and how often does that happen?

3. Who will you be working for? How well do you get along with the person who will be supervising you and the team of people you'll be working with?

4. How will you be compensated? What kind of raises are possible, and what do you need to do to qualify for one? How often are salaries increased?

When you are researching in-house jobs, whether in general or because you are interested in a specific employer, don't underestimate the power of your networks. Even if you think you don't have networks, you do. Colleges, law schools, and many large law firms all have alumni associations. Use these alumni associations to reach out to people with whom you have a built-in connection, and be sure to highlight that connection in your subject line or first message. Most people will be happy to do an informational interview with you if they have the time to do so.

Christine Morton[101] has had years of experience working in-house, and currently represents one of the most prestigious restaurant groups in the world. Being in-house suits her more than working in a firm because what she enjoys most is translating legal risks in order to help businesses make strategic moves in line with their compliance obligations. Although she enjoyed law school and understood her classes so well that she could tutor her classmates, she never got the kinds of grades that would have made her stand out to the biggest law firms. Fifteen years later, she would be diagnosed with ADHD, but at the time she did not understand the disconnect between her knowledge and her test scores.

Instead, Christine joined a small firm right after college and learned to do a mix of real estate and retail work. But the work wasn't satisfying, and she kept wondering whether private practice was the right thing for her. After a challenging pregnancy, she left her firm when her son was born. Taking that leave gave her the time she needed to recover physically and mentally from the experience of working all hours while she was expecting. It also led her to the first of two moments in her career when she had an "electric shock" of seeing a position on Craigslist that was a perfect match for her skills. It was a family-run business that needed someone who had the kind of experience working with restaurants and leasing that she had most enjoyed in practice.

When that company got rid of her division after six years, Christine considered her options. She worked with a solo practitioner for a few months, but it was a bad personal fit. Then she found what seemed like a perfect law firm, run by women who had split off from a larger firm in order to create a practice where people could wear athleisure to work. The problem, Christine says, is that "they were also sort of crazy." As with most other firms in the area, there was an intense pressure to bill seven days a week. It wasn't for her. Unfortunately, the women she had worked with saw her choice as a moral failure rather than a difference in priorities.

Christine decided that being in-house was better for her, and joined a large property management company. While she was there, she was diagnosed with ADHD, and realized that she could not enjoy her work under the conditions at that company. Through personal connections, she found another role helping a restaurant group based in Florida. Although Christine was in Washington DC, the company had no problem with her working from home and on a reduced schedule so she could have the flexibility to be with her two children when she needed to be. The only problem was that they completely failed to listen to her advice. "They would praise me for my counsel and then just go rogue and do whatever they wanted," she recalls. "There were times when I wouldn't hear from them, and I knew something was brewing." It was frustrating but comical. It was also a little lonely.

Her second electric shock moment came in 2020, when she saw an Instagram ad for the company she works for now. She knew immediately that working for this expanding restaurant group was the perfect fit for her expertise, experience, and needs as a mother. Her current role gives her the intellectual satisfaction of solving problems for a fascinating company and the flexibility to be the kind of mother that she wants to be.

Question 4: Would you be happier in a fundamentally different role within the firm?

Another question to consider is whether you need to leave the firm in order to do something fundamentally different.

Jennifer Rakstad, at White & Case, exemplifies this kind of transition within a firm. Like many of us, Jennifer went to law school because she majored in the humanities, did well on the LSAT, and wasn't sure what else to do. After clerking in Puerto Rico, she started as an associate at Mayer Brown's Chicago office. Her plan was to practice for a few years and then consider her options. Because she was passionate about diversity, she started a women's affinity group within the firm. She was also invited to work on recruiting, which she enjoyed because of the people she got to meet and work with. Eight years later, she found herself in a difficult position. She had developed an insurance practice initially, but that disappeared when the firm went through a merger and eliminated that area. She started working on ERISA cases instead, which was less engaging. By the time she was supposed to go up for partnership, she had no interest in building a case for herself as a partner.

Instead of going up for partner, she took a different route: taking on a newly created role helping other mid-level attorneys with their professional development. Jennifer had always enjoyed the interpersonal aspects of her work on recruiting and the women's initiative more than her billable practice. Around that time, another attorney had created a new role for himself as the "dean of associates" at Mayer Brown. He asked Jennifer to consider joining his team within the firm as a "career development attorney." This was a much more interesting option than partnership or leaving the firm entirely, so she accepted.

While Jennifer was on maternity leave the following year, the "dean of associates" left Mayer Brown. Jennifer saw an opportunity to expand her role and started networking with other career development professionals in law firms. All of them were in what they considered their second careers. Jennifer got the advice that "in the field of professional development, you can focus on recruiting, training, or coaching," and she wanted to coach. She persuaded the firm to sponsor her coaching certification through the Hudson Institute, and became one of the first internal coaches at a large law firm. When she attended certification sessions at Hudson, in California, she would fold in visits to the firm's West Coast offices to mentor associates there.

Over time, Jennifer's role changed and grew. She started a group coaching program for associates who had similar interests and needs. One group helped senior associates figure out their career goals, while another group focused on coaching associates who were preparing their case for partnership. Mayer Brown began to offer broader coaching options, which in turn encouraged their lawyers to be more open about their interests. She witnessed the firm's growing acceptance of the fact that not all associates want to progress to partnership and growing support for a wider range of paths.

After several years, Jennifer moved into a new role at White & Case, where she now oversees the learning and development offerings for non-partner lawyers and business services professionals for its offices in the Americas region. Her team offers training and coaching for both attorneys and nonlegal staff on topics including professionalism, imposter syndrome, project management, people management, and business development. She is one of the most sought after leaders in law firm learning and development worldwide.

Jennifer's advice to anyone considering a different role within their law firm is to start with a step back. If your firm doesn't have an in-house career coach, she recommends taking time to do the kind of reflection outlined in Chapter 7. She took a few weeks off to think about what she wanted before accepting the associate development role at Mayer Brown. She found that time and distance invaluable in giving her the perspective she needed for such a significant change.

Question 5: Would you be happier with a less traditional career path?

You don't have to have a long-term strategy to end up more than satisfied over the long term with the way your career evolves. While lawyers tend to be especially good at strategic analysis, there is much to be said for making decisions that fit your needs at the time without worrying about how they will look in the future. In fact, there is no way to know exactly how your decisions now will look to potential employers in the future. Much will depend on how you frame it and on what those employers are looking for.

Lori Fein's career has shapeshifted over time, in line with her priorities and the changing needs of her family. The mother of five daughters, Lori now has a hybrid career. She spends about sixty percent of her time working as a senior attorney for the New Jersey office of a firm based in Pittsburgh. She spends the remaining time consulting on development and fundraising for a foreign university.

Dividing her professional time between practicing law and consulting makes sense for Lori in several ways. For both family and religious reasons, it is important that her employers allow for more flexibility than either a larger law firm or a full-time development role is likely to offer. Because both employers know that she works part time, she has a great deal of flexibility as to how she schedules her work for each one.

More importantly, balancing law with consulting is more rewarding, both personally and financially, than either would be alone. Her law firm role allows her to use her problem-solving skills and legal knowledge while providing a stable income. Her consulting role allows her to use her brilliant interpersonal skills to develop support for an institution she cares deeply about. Lori is a talented connector of people, and consulting allows her to use that talent for a purpose she values. The symbiosis of skills, values, and different types of rewards works well for her right now.

But it wasn't always this way. Lori started off on a more traditional career path. After graduating from Columbia Law School, she started as an associate at Skadden Arps in New York. Although she initially had wanted to do litigation, she landed in their antitrust group instead. When her husband got a job with a federal agency in Washington, she moved to Skadden's D.C. office. Being at the branch office felt different from being in the center of things, however, and she left Skadden for what was then Wilmer Cutler & Pickering. Although she hoped to restart her litigation work, Wilmer was soon engaged in a huge antitrust case. Excited by her antitrust experience, they put her on it. Around this time, she had her first child. "Nothing at work was as interesting to me as watching this baby," she recalls, and she took a year's leave to be with her daughter. By the time she returned to Wilmer, Lori was a 5th year associate. She finally had the opportunity to do litigation, but effectively had no prior litigation experience, so it was especially challenging. Add to this that she never enjoyed civil procedure, and her cases were procedure-intensive. The parts of litigation practice that seemed easy for other associates at her level did not come naturally to her.

Within a short period of time, there was more disruption. She had a miscarriage, and then her grandmother passed away. She kept working long enough to help pay off her own student loans and most of her husband's loans. Soon after the birth of her second child, her husband joined a firm and Lori decided to leave Wilmer. She had two more girls, and did some part time trusts and estates work for a small DC firm as the preschool and private school tuition bills started to come in. Eventually, she found herself with four children in a two-bedroom apartment, which was becoming increasingly uncomfortable as the kids grew. It was around then that her husband was recruited to a bank in New York, not far from where most of Lori's family lived.

As much as Lori values being a mother, she did not want to give up working in some role. She did not always love being a lawyer, but it was her most marketable professional experience. As she was considering what to do, she became pregnant again, and her grandmother decided to move into their new house in

New Jersey to "help take care of the girls." That is how Lori found herself responsible for five girls and a 90-year-old woman. Around this time, the stock market crashed, and it was hard for anyone to find a job. For the next few years, Lori put together a patchwork of legal consulting work, much of it unpaid. She did some consulting for nonprofits, helped friends of friends with wills, and helped cousins with various kinds of legal advice.

In 2013, a personal tragedy compelled her to stop waiting for the perfect career to appear. Lori wanted to contribute to the world in different ways than she had as a mother and to model working outside the home for her five daughters. There were financial needs as well. Because the girls went to private religious school, and college now loomed for the older girls, tuition fees were another reason to go back to work.

What was less clear was the kind of work she should do. Practicing law wasn't as compelling to her as public policy and advocacy work, and would have required more of a time commitment than she could make. She put together a resume highlighting the skills she had used in consulting while her kids were younger and circulated it to friends. Through her network, she landed the position of Executive Director of an educational nonprofit not far from her home. Although it was a full-time role, she worked fewer hours than a "part-time" job at a law firm would have required. She also had more control over her schedule. She was still away from home often enough that her daughters learned to take more responsibility at home than they had had to before, an unexpected benefit of going back to work.

That first nonprofit leadership role led to another, and eventually Lori was offered a part-time consulting role that paid as much as most full time roles. A year later, as her oldest daughter was applying to some of the most expensive colleges in the country, she started looking at law firms again. It surprised her that her prestigious college and law school names still impressed employers after so many years away from practice. Through a fortuitous mix-up, the full-time job Lori had applied for morphed into a part-time position before she accepted the offer. That allowed Lori to keep her part-time consulting work and take on a new role as a senior associate.

Having been away from law practice for over a decade, Lori valued the opportunity to start at a lower seniority level when she started working for her firm. Starting at the associate level gave her a chance to re-learn deposition, legal research, and drafting skills. It wasn't long before she was promoted, but those initial months learning alongside people who were 20 years younger than her allowed her to feel more comfortable easing back into the practice of law.

Lori's advice to lawyers who want to follow a nontraditional path is to use whatever connections you have to develop more connections. She recommends approaching people who have posted on LinkedIn or social media about topics you find interesting. Asking people whether they can spare ten or 15 minutes to talk with you will often result in a conversation. "Most people are happy to give advice and enjoy having an eager listener," she points out.

To make the most of those conversations, remember to ask for a second point of connection. Asking "who else do you think I should talk to?" or whether your contact would be willing to introduce you to a third person usually leads to another helpful conversation. If you are worried that you are bothering them, don't be. As Lori points out, they will say no if they need to.

Asking these questions while you are still at your law firm provides you with the maximum amount of information and leverage. You have an infinite number of options, even when you feel hemmed in by a practice that isn't working for you. And as you'll see in the next chapter, there are many other strategies for navigating the challenges of caregiving in the next chapter of your professional life.

Building Bridges Instead of Burning Them

If you do choose to leave your law firm, make sure you do it the right way. If you have spent time in a mid-size or larger law firm, you have almost certainly seen "this is my last day" emails. You may even have sent one or two yourself. In these emails, the soon-to-be-former associates express something about their time at the firm and sometimes let people know how they can be reached in the future. Associates will sometimes use these emails as a last opportunity to get things off their chest before they leave. They have nothing left to lose, they think, so they might as well tell it like it is on their way out the door. It's a common yet cringeworthy scenario. It's also a big mistake on the part of the sender, and one that is easy to avoid.

Cathartic goodbye emails are a waste of resources. Sending a snarky final email to co-workers has never changed the behavior of any co-workers in the history of either email or co-workers. Worse, it can make you seem petty, which is not the way you want to be remembered.

Leaving a firm provides an invaluable opportunity to do something good for yourself and your professional future. If you are going to say goodbye to your co-workers in a final email, use that opportunity wisely. Joseph Gerstel's final email to his Big Law colleagues is an excellent example of the right way to leave.

When Joseph decided to leave Davis Polk in order to start his own educational event planning company, he wanted to make the most of his exit. Gerstel, founder and CEO of Get Some Class, had created a series of online classes for employers to offer as a way of helping their employees stay connected and engaged during the Covid-19 pandemic. For each class, employees would receive a kit in the mail that would include themed snacks and all the materials they would need. His first clients were big law firms, a sector he knew well from being an associate. As his client list grew to include tech companies and management consulting firms, he realized that he needed to walk away from his law firm job in order to grow his startup.

Joseph saw his last communication with his colleagues as an opportunity to build bridges. His goodbye email gave him a platform from which he could reach more than 2,000 lawyers in the firm, many of whom might be important contacts for his growing business. So he did something extraordinary. He hired a sand artist to make a short video that depicted his transition from law school to the Manhattan offices of Davis Polk. In the video, stick figures drawn in the shifting sand come together to support an arrow with an upwards trajectory over the skyscrapers. Then a frame emerges over the collective work, and another figure waves goodbye as the video closes out. It was unmistakably personal, detailed, creative and thoughtful, designed to make a positive impression on everyone who saw it. And that impression could only help Joseph when he reconnected with his former co-workers in the future.

The responses to Joseph's goodbye message were heartwarming. People he had never worked with wrote to him to say that they wished they had known him better. Congratulations and well wishes flooded his inbox from senior partners and counsel across all of Davis Polk's departments. He left his entire firm with a positive impression, which is rarely the outcome of a goodbye email.

Whether you should stay or go is one of the most challenging decisions a law firm lawyer can make. Staying doesn't have to mean suffering, if you can find ways to advocate for yourself successfully and if what is making you unhappy can be changed within the firm. But if you decide to leave your law firm, we've got you covered. There are an infinite number of realistic and rewarding career options for former lawyers. We will help you choose the one(s) that are the best fit for you and make the transition as seamless as possible.

CHAPTER 7

Redesign Strategies for Leaving the Law

"I feel like law is similar to design. When I was in a conference room negotiating, I had a blast. It's creative, it's problem solving."[102]

—Dana Lynch, lawyer turned interior designer

LEAVING THE LAW can feel overwhelming. Impossible. Impractical. But it is not. In this chapter, we'll give you the most effective strategies to help make every part of the process easier. Drawing on the wisdom of other former lawyers as well as our own experiences, we will help you manage what can seem at first like an unmanageable change.

As we have discussed in previous chapters, it can be hard enough deciding that you need to make a change in your professional life. How much needs to change, and what a meaningful change would look like, are even harder questions to answer. We are not big fans of quitting your job without a plan, although one of us definitely did that just before one of the most serious financial crises of the 21st century.

It is absolutely critical to figure out what is bothering you about your work situation before you make major decisions about what to do next. Moving from one law firm to another law firm, for example, often does not result in the kinds of improvement that associates expect it to. So, too, beware of moving from a law firm to nonprofit work, or to in-house work, when there hasn't been enough analysis about what the root of the problem was at the law firm in the first place. For purposes of this chapter, we'll assume that you need a game plan for leaving the law itself.

When you leave the law, you are in excellent company, but it may not feel that way at first. Although there are dizzying numbers of former lawyers who have gone through successful career transitions, it can feel like you are the only one who is crazy enough to contemplate giving up all of that material success and prestige. The "alumni association" for former lawyers is not well defined or even visible to most lawyers and law students who are still grappling with how much they want to practice law. And that isolation complicates the process of leaving. For most lawyers, walking away from something they have trained to do for years is either a struggle or the inevitable result of burnout.

But you are not alone. And many of the former lawyers who have struggled with their own transitions have advice that should make every part of leaving the law easier. In this chapter, we consolidate some of our best advice and that of other ex-lawyers about every stage of the transition process.

Devoting Time to Think

When Liz was a lawyer, she spent a lot of time squelching her misery. At random times during the day, she would start to feel nauseous or furious or unbearably sad, and then she would have to suppress all of those feelings and get right back to whatever billable thing she was doing. Her emotions started manifesting as stomach aches when she came into the office every morning. That continued until she started carving out small periods of time—five minutes here, ten minutes there—to start thinking about getting out. It was not easy to make that time or to face those feelings. Practicing law is a time-consuming, time-dependent business. If you can barely find time to have lunch, how can you find time to think beyond the next case or project? And when you do, how can you make that time productive, instead of just venting about how horrible you feel?

One strategy for carving out time is to schedule it for yourself, as you would for any external commitment. Think of yourself as your own client. Putting a ten-minute block on your calendar is a step towards making space for your own thoughts. If other people have access to that calendar, you can label it something vague like a "meeting" or "conference." Every time you make space for your own personal and professional development, you reinforce that internal sense of agency that so many of us lose in the legal profession. You underscore for yourself that your own thoughts and feelings matter in your career choices. Blocking out that time on your calendar at least once a week, and ideally a few times a week, will help you make more progress than waiting for a big block of time to open up.

So what would you do in ten minutes, or five? There are a lot of small bites you can take in that time that could make a difference to your own thinking about your professional options over time. Most of them involve brainstorming or responding to a specific prompt, ideally in writing. If you can write longhand in a journal or notebook, that will be even more productive than typing on a screen. Here are some options for a ten-minute reflective break:

1. What experiences or interactions have you had in the past 24-48 hours that were personally rewarding? What small parts of the last day or two felt not just like a break, but like a joy?

2. Who is one of your role models, and why? What is it specifically that you admire about that person?

3. If you could do any job and be good at it, and you did not have to worry about money, what would you do?

4. When you were younger, what did you want to do when you grew up? Is that career still interesting to you?

5. Think of one person you know whose job you want to learn more about. What do you think it takes to be successful at that job? Is it something you would like to explore further?

6. Are there any other jobs, or fields, that you wish you knew more about? Do they have professional organizations that you can find online?

You may also have your own career research agenda that you can break into small blocks of time. Setting aside these mini-breaks for your own reflection is an easy way to start taking action about a possible career transition without a major commitment of resources or risk. Once you are in the habit of giving yourself more time to think, even sporadically, the process of leaving the law for a better-fitting career becomes much more feasible.

The "Life After Law" Four-Step Process

There is, in essence, a recipe for making a career change from law into something much more rewarding for you personally. It requires setting aside time to think differently about what makes you truly happy, and it requires introspection. It also requires some external research, which lawyers tend to be better at than people in most other professions. And it can be done on your own timeline. You don't have to leave your law firm before you start identifying your next career.

In the next stage of your career transition, you will focus on exploring only the careers that make the most of your preferred skills. Brainstorming about potential career options is often the most difficult and most frustrating part of the alternative career search for lawyers. Internet searches for "former lawyer" and "what can I do with a law degree" are generally the result of wanting an external source of job titles that lawyers can do. This is not a great strategy. Lawyers can do pretty much anything. What you want, instead, is to come up with something that you should do because you would be wonderful at it and it would bring you joy.

The most important part of leaving the law is paying attention to what skills you enjoy using the most. The introspective work of considering what aspects of your legal career (if any) have brought you the most joy is the key to finding another career that you will enjoy even more. Think of this a different way: finding another career that allows you to use the skills you developed as a lawyer will only make you as happy as using those skills does, regardless of the context. You may be a talented advocate for your clients, but if you do not enjoy advocacy, using your persuasive skills in another context like marketing or sales is not going to be more rewarding than what you were doing as a lawyer. You have to enjoy the skills you are using in your work, intrinsically, to be happy at work. The key question is not what you are good at, regardless of the professional context in which you use those skills. It is this: what skills do you most enjoy using? What do you get the most enjoyment out of being good at?

In *Life After Law: Finding Work You Love with the JD You Have*, Liz described a four-step process for a successful transition out of law. She developed this process after talking with hundreds of happy ex-lawyers and reflecting on what their paths all had in common. In the years since that book was published, we have counseled many more former lawyers and we have seen the process work, again and again. Here are the four steps.

Step 1: Identify What You ENJOY Being Good at.

The first step in this process is to figure out what skills you already have that bring you joy when you use them. You know what you're good at, right? Maybe you went into the legal profession because you are a great writer (or at least you were, before you had to write all those briefs or draft those contracts). But there is a critical difference between being good at writing and being happy while writing. The difference between just working and enjoying work turns on that distinction.

Let's say your primary objective is to have a personally rewarding work life. That's our goal for you, too. If you don't enjoy doing your work, it doesn't matter all that much if you are good at it. People can praise you all day long and pay you exorbitant sums of money, but if your work is slowly crushing your soul, you won't be able to sustain that forever. And you shouldn't. Life is too short to hate your work.

The primary question, then, is what skills you want to get paid to use at work every day. What talents do you have that make you feel great, even if you have never been paid to use them specifically? One way to think about this is to consider when you feel a sense of what the late Mihaly Csikszentmihályi called flow: an optimal sense of immersion in what you are doing. When does time seem to stop for you? What kinds of activities that bring you the greatest sense of contentment and reward?

Many of the lawyers we have worked with were stumped by this. It's not the same as figuring out the kinds of skills and strengths that come up on typical personality tests. Answering this question requires you to think about happiness, which a lot of lawyers instinctively disassociate from work.

Here's another way to think this through: can you think of a time in your life when you were completely absorbed in what you were doing? This could be a time when you were in high school, in college, or maybe something you were doing more recently either at or outside of work. Write down a brief sketch of everything you can remember about that time. Now think of another anecdote involving a different time when you were caught up in some activity and lost track of time because it was so engaging. Once you have a few of these anecdotes written down, or even just in your mind, you may be able to see a pattern. Is there some common thread among these stories? What skills or talents were you using when you felt a sense of flow?

Another way to appreciate what you enjoy being good at is to turn to the people who know you best. Turn to your friends and to the family you are closest to. Ask them: what do you think I am good at? What do you see as my natural talents? Importantly, you should not ask them what they think you should be doing professionally. That's not helpful at this particular stage of the process. What you hear from the people you *don't* work with can be especially enlightening. But remember, what you are good at is not the same as, and not as useful in career transitions, as what you enjoy being good at. It's the latter that you want to focus on identifying here.

In our experience, people who gravitate toward law school tend to have at least one of the following skills:

1. Writing
2. Public speaking
3. Advocacy
4. Counseling
5. Complex problem solving
6. Persuasion
7. Logical analysis
8. Pattern recognition

This isn't an exhaustive list, of course. But the important thing to notice is this: these skills which are so common in lawyers are all valuable outside of law. *None of these skills is unique to the legal profession.* You just have to focus on the skills that you especially enjoy being good at. The next stage of the process involves applying those skills in one or more alternative careers. You will find a much more detailed explanation of how to reframe your existing legal skills in new ways in the next chapter.

If you were hoping that we would tell you to figure out what interests you, we're sorry to disappoint you. What you're interested in can be a secondary driver of your career choice, but it should not be the first concern. In our experience, interests are not nearly as productive as skills when it comes to developing new career options. What you are interested in may well be relevant to the fields in which you want to use your unique preferred skills, but you should not base your entire search on those interests.

Consider this as an example. Let's say you love books. Maybe you love reading them, talking about them, collecting them, or all of the above. If your interest in books was driving your career transition, you might think about working for a publisher or a bookstore. Great! But how would you convince a publisher or a bookstore to hire you? What value would you add to that business? If you're thinking "Well, I do know a lot about the law," you are heading in the direction of artificially limiting your career options to working in the general counsel's office if one exists. That is the wrong direction if you are looking for a more fundamental shift. Similarly, if you are interested in sports, you aren't likely to be able to score a job with a team, a sports network, or any other business in the sports field unless you can show them why you would be a valuable hire.

Sure, you could start with an entry level job, but you don't have to. In fact, the fear of starting from the bottom all over again is one of the main reasons that people fear career change to begin with. But if you capitalize on the skills you have already developed, you can make more of a lateral move. You do not have to start from scratch if you reframe and repurpose your existing skills for a new field, which you'll do in step three of this process. If you can demonstrate that you are an expert in managing, or in educating and training people, then your chances of getting a more substantive job in that field increase exponentially. And that starts with figuring out which of your skills you want to showcase.

Step 2: Identify Other Professions That Value Those Skills.

Once you have identified a few preferred skills that you can envision getting paid for, the next step is to identify specific careers to explore. Figuring out what your new career options are, given your preferred skills, is the hardest part of the process for many people. It can feel impossible to think about what other kinds of jobs, in entirely unfamiliar industries, require. In the immortal words of Richard Scarry, what do other people do all day?

Fortunately, it is easier now than it has ever been before to learn more about other fields and careers within those fields. One way to do this is to look at examples of what other people with similar skills have done after practicing law. We recommend following podcasts and blogs that feature profiles of former lawyers. One of our favorites is Sarah Cottrell's "Former Lawyer" series. *Life After Law* also features the stories of many former lawyers, grouped by the kinds of skills they ended up using in their next and more rewarding careers.

Another way to figure out some potential alternative careers is to talk widely with your network about the skills you want to focus on. When you tell people that you want to leave the law, we guarantee you that 99% of them will have no idea what to tell you, other than hopefully to offer their support. But when you tell people that you are looking for new ways to use your persuasive advocacy skills, for example, or that you are looking for new opportunities to counsel people about major business decisions or strategies, it is much more likely that you will get useful suggestions.

When you have a potential alternative career in mind, the single most important thing to do is to have a frank conversation with someone who is actually in that field. By "conversation," we mean an informational interview that involves you asking questions and letting the other person do about 90% of the talking. You can think of this as kicking the tires of your next career. There is nothing like talking with someone who has the actual experience of doing the job you think you yourself may want to commit to for the foreseeable future. Think about it: would you ever recommend that someone become a lawyer without a realistic grasp of what law practice can involve? Our best advice for networking in a post-COVID world follows in Chapter 9.

Approaching someone for an informational interview is much easier when you have either a personal connection or something in common, such as an alma mater or a mutual interest in something you can mention right away. Ideally, you will keep the length of your interview to 30 minutes or less, and come prepared with specific questions that will help you make the most of your time. There is so much you can learn about most people's education and work history on LinkedIn that you won't need to waste time asking about those things.

Instead, focus on asking open-ended questions about things that are less easy to figure out from an online search, and will help you evaluate whether this field fits you well. Effective basic questions might include:

- What do you like best, and what do you like least, about what you do?

- What do you wish you had known more about when you went into this field?

- What skills are most important to do excellent work in this field?

Conversely, here are some questions you should *never* ask in an informational interview:

- Do you think I would be successful in this field?

- Do you know of any job openings right now?

- Do you have any feedback on my resume?

If you're hesitant to approach people for informational interviews, don't be. Most people are flattered when you show an interest in them, as long as you are not asking them for a favor or, even worse, for a job. Most people like to talk about themselves and to help someone else in the process. If you can make the informational interview short, sweet, and easy on your subject, you're likely to learn something valuable.

Finally, don't forget that one of your goals in every informational interview is to get an additional contact. Two great closing questions are "Can you suggest anyone else I should talk to?" and "May I please use your name when I contact them?" Every step in your networking process should expand your network if possible.

Step 3: Translate Your Skills Into the New Profession's Language.
Once you have a sense of which alternative careers have potential, given the skills you most enjoy using, it's time to apply for some jobs. Are you going to use your legal resume? No, you're not. If you don't want to apply for a law job, you don't want to use a lawyer's resume without making some adjustments for your new audience. The best way to get noticed in a new field is to make

sure you speak their language. The best way to do this is to write a new resume that highlights your skills and translates them into the language of the field you're trying to enter.

One of the most common mistakes lawyers make when they are switching careers is to skip this step. Using your standard resume to apply for a job outside of law is a low risk way to put out feelers, but it is likely to fail. That doesn't mean that you are not qualified for the job you are applying for. It just means that you haven't made your qualifications clear enough. Unlike other lawyers, people outside of the legal field have little appreciation for what is involved in practicing law. They are extremely unlikely to infer that your years of taking depositions makes you an active listener who is good at conducting interviews and doing interpersonal research. They are far more likely to stop at "depositions" and delete your resume from their database.

It is a much better practice to revise your resume by adopting the words used in the job description. If you can adopt the terminology of a new field in describing your skills and experience, you are on your way to speaking their language. Ideally, you'll create a new resume for each job you apply for, so that your resume is as "narrowly tailored" as possible.

Step 4: Refine and Reframe Your Options.

Once you know what you want to do, you're done, right? Not so fast. You will probably still wonder whether you should really take the leap into another career. After all, most lawyers don't have much professional experience doing anything else, having trained for at least three years in this one specialized way of thinking.

For most careers, there are ways to mitigate the risk that you will regret your choice. The first is to get more information directly from people in these careers, in the form of more in-depth informational interviewing than you may already have done. The second is to take the new gig out for a test drive, for example, through an internship or a trial period. For more on these risk mitigation techniques, see our discussion in Chapter 12.

Remember, too, that none of your decisions is permanent. If you take a step in a particular direction and something feels off, you can pivot. You can always change direction. In our years of helping other former lawyers find more rewarding careers, one of the most common misconceptions we have seen is that the full picture of their next career has to be clear before they can make any progress at all. It is far more common for former lawyers to take a step or two along a new path, and then find that the next steps appear in front of them. You don't need to have a whole new career mapped out before you start taking steps away from a career that diminishes your sense of self. Taking the small steps, and the small risks, is the best way to make the larger decisions possible.

Other Ways to Find Your Next Best Career

As strongly as we believe in this four-step process, there are other productive methods for narrowing the scope of career options that could be right for you personally. There are two other methods we recommend in particular.

Another method we recommend using to identify the kinds of jobs that are most likely to be rewarding is the "Flower" exercise developed by Richard Bolles in his classic book *What Color Is Your Parachute?* Bolles also calls this exercise "that one piece of paper" because it consolidates a lot of important input about your unique preferences on a single page. The purpose of this exercise is to bring together the results of your introspective thinking about several different aspects of your career search. These include your preferred strengths, preferred environments and colleagues, preferred locations, and ideal goals and purposes. That is a lot of information to develop in advance of doing the exercise, and Bolles' book guides you through every step. It is a classic for a reason.

This "Flower" exercise can help all lawyers who are struggling with how to organize their thoughts about career transitions. Its genius is in the spatial organization of the most important factors. In Bolles' flower diagram, there is a central space surrounded by six petal-shaped spaces. In the central space, which takes up about half of the page, you write down several of your preferred strengths, which he calls transferable skills, in order of their importance to you. That forms the center of the flower. Radiating out from that central space are the six rounded petal spaces of the flower. In these spaces, Bolles recommends that you write down (1) the values, goals and/or purposes you would most like to work on; (2) the unique knowledge that you want your ideal employer to focus on, (3) the kinds of people and environments that you would most enjoy working in, (4) the working conditions that matter the most to you, (5) your ideal, or minimum, pay grade and seniority level, and (6) the geographic locations you most want to target.

Collecting all of this information on a single sheet of paper, using this graphic design, is an ingenious way of bringing together a lot of different inputs. It helps you avoid the "whack a mole" feeling of having different factors and concerns pop up at the most inconvenient times during the process of exploring alternative careers.

Another way of framing the key features of your next career is Taylor Pearson's paint drop method. The idea behind this method is that truly successful people have unusual expertise and skills sets that are in high demand. While some people derive success from being among the best in the world at one thing, like playing the violin or swimming, more people become successful by combining two to four skills. The paint drop method helps you visualize what these two to four skills might look like for you.

It works like this: visualize a wide paint brush heavy with paint that you drag horizontally against a wall. Paint will probably drip vertically down the wall in an uneven pattern as you move the brush across the wall. Most of these drips will only be an inch or two long, but some will run longer down the wall where the paint is heavier. The broad horizontal stroke, Pearson suggests, represents the timeline of your school and work life so far. The shorter drops represent your knowledge and interests generally, which will vary a bit from topic to topic. Maybe you enjoyed studying art or know a lot about anthropology because those are interests you have picked up along the way, but they are not things you feel deeply about or have a special talent for.

The longer drips, however, represent the stronger skills and talents that may provide more value in your career. Combining a few of these greater strengths in your next career will provide the basis for success. But how do you identify these greater strengths? Pearson boils it down to this question: "What can you do well, that you also find interesting, and that people will pay for?" The first question is what you are good at: in other words, your skills. These include what your friends, colleagues, bosses, and teachers have praised you for.

The second question is what you find most engaging. As we explain in the first step of our own process above, one way to figure out what you love being good at is to think about when you lose track of time. Feeling a sense of flow, or engagement, is a good sign that you are enjoying what you do. The overlap between those two things—what you are good at and what you enjoy—is what you should find a way to do professionally.

You can identify these signature strengths by finding overlap among the skills you have, the things you find most enjoyable and engaging, and the skills that have some kind of market value. This is similar to our framework for identifying your preferred skills, with the added criteria of considering the potential financial rewards for those skills.

As you can see, there are methods to what may at first seem like the madness of leaving the law. What all the methods we describe in this chapter have in common is that they demand a combination of introspection and external research, and that they are unique to you. Nobody can, or should, just tell you what your career options are because you went to law school. Your law degree does not limit your professional options. What should define those options instead includes your own unique skills, interests, prefer-ences, and assessments. Using these methods, you will be able to design your own career transition, moving into work that is uniquely perfect for you.

CHAPTER 8

Leveraging Your Legal Experience Instead of Discarding It

*"My worst day as an artist is still better than
my best day as a lawyer."*[103]

–Nathan Sawaya, former lawyer and internationally
renowned Lego Brick Artist

ONE OF THE MOST COMMON concerns lawyers have about making a career change is that they fear that they won't be able to succeed in any other career. More specifically, they believe that they don't have the skills necessary to do anything other than practice law. In this chapter, we will explain why that is never true.

Lawyers, in general, have an artificially narrow view of the value and transferability of their skills. For most of us, law school is where the sense of professional isolation begins. In our first days of training, we are taught that there are specialized rules and names for almost everything related to the legal system. The fact that there are Federal Rules of Civil Procedure alone is mind-bogglingly specific. Most law schools dedicate an entire course to Civil Procedure in the first year, so that students can be at least familiar with the gamut of particular requirements for every aspect of going to court. We are not going to suggest that knowing the Federal Rules of Civil Procedure is a helpful skill in any other career. But the skills law students use in learning and applying those rules are very useful in other professions, as we describe in more detail below.

Law school is a powerfully insulating experience. The classes law students take relate to their professional development as lawyers because it is, after all, a trade school. Although classes like Moot Court might train students in the public speaking and persuasive advocacy skills that could be helpful in presenting to a board of directors or a school committee, those alternative contexts are not the focus of the class. The focus of Moot Court is on presenting oral arguments before a judge or judicial panel. The subject matter of moot court exercises is generally a specific hypothetical case. But the law students who excel at oral arguments have developed skills that they can use in a far broader range of contexts than just hearings and trials. There is just no reason and no opportunity to underscore how useful those skills can be in other contexts during law school.

The same is true in other core law school classes. Legal Writing classes require students to adjust the writing skills they may have developed in high school and college and adapt to the format of briefs and motions. Students learn to analyze and discuss case law. These courses emphasize the law-specific nature of their subject matter. In doing so, they tend to obscure the fact that students are honing their analytical and persuasive writing skills in general. Yes, the subject matter is law and the primary materials are cases, but there is still more generally transferrable skill being developed in these courses than most law students realize. Law schools have no incentive to point that out, but it remains true.

Traditionally, law schools have not explicitly acknowledged that the skills they help students develop may be useful in other professions. And why should they? The emphasis is on preparation for a career that requires a JD, and so law students generally go through their three years of graduate education with those professional blinders on. The range of future career options is cabined by the substantive practice of law, ranging from firms to public service to nonprofits, but not extending much beyond those options. An increasing number of law schools offer assistance to alumni who are considering non-legal careers. For the past several decades, however, those alumni have often felt like pariahs or misfits in the general population of law school graduates. The idea that some people who go to law school might be better off not practicing any form of law has been, for the most part, anathema.

Our professional blinders usually stay on after law school graduation. Once they leave law school, lawyers spend years, sometimes decades, developing specialized knowledge about procedures and case law that are relevant to their work. This post-JD experience further narrows their sense of what else they might do professionally. They have become subject-matter experts, usually in a particular geographic area. Given the value of their expertise, they would not feel as comfortable doing anything else, anywhere else. For example, a family law attorney who specializes in high net worth divorce cases in Massachusetts presumably has a good knowledge of the procedures involved in getting divorced in that state as well as the case law that family court judges are likely to rely on in several common conflict scenarios. That specialized expertise allows the lawyer to provide valuable advice to her clients without doing a lot of legal research, for the most part. Of course, in order to develop that expertise, the lawyer has spent years doing that research and following those procedures, and can now capitalize on that experience.

Those specialized areas are relatively narrow and not immediately transferrable. Most lawyers would not even feel comfortable acting as lawyers for themselves in cases where they don't have the appropriate expertise. The family law expert is going to turn to someone else in her network to handle a real estate transaction, a complex contract negotiation, or a copyright registration. This, of course, is one of the reasons that it is so frustrating for lawyers when friends and family ask them for legal advice about something in which they don't specialize. To someone who doesn't understand how different each area of law is and how different the laws in different states can be, that can seem like a reasonable request. Doctors often face the same problem, we are told.

The combination of law school and the specialized experience many lawyers develop after law school can create a false sense of professional scarcity. The key to leveraging your legal experience in a non-legal career search is to **separate skills from substantive knowledge**. Lawyers develop both skills and substantive knowledge from the first weeks of law school, and we rarely think of separating them. This is the point at which that separation, that distinction between the substance and the procedure, becomes the source of enormous career potential. We believe that the substance of most jobs is something you can learn. The development of skills, however, is much harder to establish.

The fact that skills are more important than substantive knowledge has never been clearer. In many fields, the substantive knowledge relevant to that profession becomes obsolete over time due to a confluence of societal, cultural, and technological changes. As substance-specific knowledge decreases in importance, the ability to demonstrate key skills becomes even more essential. And lawyers are likely to have many of these key skills already, given the range of their training in law school and in practice.

Repurposing Legal Skills: One Example

Liz's experience in both of her post-law jobs provides great examples of this phenomenon. In her first legal career, Liz was a Big Law litigator, representing Fortune 500 companies in patent litigation and other complex business cases. She knew something substantive about patent law and about the other areas of law that had been important for the cases she worked on. For every case, in every new jurisdiction, there was a new set of information to learn, so her substantive knowledge of patent law increased over time. It was useful solely in patent litigation, and not really transferrable anywhere else.

Her skill set, however, was and is different. She had learned how to do legal research in law school, building on the general research skills she enjoyed using as a History and Literature major in college. She had learned how to talk productively with senior executives in practice. She developed the skills necessary to put those executives at ease in part through working with and advising senior counsel. She also improved her ability to talk with busy people in high status positions by preparing dozens of executives for depositions. She had also learned how to manage complicated projects by taking on case management as she went up the associate ladder and eventually made partner. In addition, she had helped to organize mentoring networks for women lawyers at her firms. Setting up those networks had required her to work with the most senior women in the firm, many of whom worked in other cities and other offices. All of those skills—research, counseling, interviewing, networking, and project management—were separable from her legal experience and transferrable to a new career.

The ability to advocate for her clients in court was perhaps the most important transferrable skill Liz used in getting her first post-law job. She had learned of a part-time position serving as the Executive Director of an angel investment firm focusing on women entrepreneurs. It sounded like the perfect job for her given her family needs, since she had a toddler at the time. It was flexible in its hours and offered enough compensation to cover the day care she would need in order to take the job on. More importantly, the job description sounded wonderful: work with high net-worth investors to help coordinate the evaluation of and possible investment in some innovative start-ups with at least one woman in a leadership role.

Had Liz used her "Lawyer CV" without any reframing, she would not have gotten the Executive Director job. There was nothing on her traditional law CV that would have persuaded that angel investment firm to hire her. Did they care that she had successfully represented this or that company in this or that circuit? Of course not. But with some careful, and honest, reframing, she could highlight the value of what she had done in her legal career that might translate into qualifications for this new position at an angel investment firm.

To do this, Liz broke down the skills that she thought would make someone successful in the job she wanted. First, the Executive Director would need to be comfortable working with extremely wealthy investors. Most of these investors would be women, so it helped to have experience working with senior women in business. She drew on her experience setting up women's mentoring networks to underscore how well she would be able to work with the women investors this organization relied on. She also drew on her experience listening to and advising in-house counsel for her clients when she was in private practice. All of those "legal" experiences had helped her develop personal relationship skills that could be useful in working with angel investors as a non-lawyer.

Another part of the role of the Executive Director was to set up and coordinate investment analysis meetings, as well as opportunities for the entrepreneurs to make their pitches. There were periodic investor meetings to organize and workshops for entrepreneurs to create. Liz knew she could do this because of her experience managing cases and setting up witness preparation meetings. The substance of the projects was different, to be sure, but the project management skills were essentially the same. Liz just had to recharacterize "case management" as "project management," which is really what it is.

The Executive Director was also tasked with doing some amount of pulling together information that would help the investors evaluate the entrepreneurs who were doing their pitches. For the most part, the investors themselves did the analysis, but the Executive Director would need to supplement their work on occasion or contribute in other ways to their decision-making process. For this part of the job, Liz could draw on her research skills. Yes, it had been decades since she had researched anything other than law as part of her career, but she had the general skills necessary to do that part of the Executive Director job well enough.

Once she developed the confidence that she had the skills necessary to do the job, Liz had to demonstrate those skills on her CV and in a cover letter well enough to get in the door. She rewrote her CV from top to bottom, emphasizing the verbs that would represent the skills that mattered most for this particular job: managed, researched, advised, organized. She took out the verbs that would sound like radio static to the angel investment firm: deposed, argued, briefed, and won. She created a new CV that was tailored specifically for this job opportunity. This tailored CV showcased the skills that she would transfer from the context of litigation to the world of angel investment. She made it easy for her target employer to see the value of what she had done previously and to understand how that previous experience qualified her for the job she now wanted.

What Liz did <u>not</u> have was any substantive knowledge whatsoever of angel investing. She wasn't actually sure what an angel investor was, to be honest. This, however, she could and did learn by reading—OK, skimming—a book about angel investing and venture capital the day before her interview. She learned enough to be conversant about this kind of funding during the interview. Had she been asked how extensive her knowledge of angel investing was, she would have answered honestly. But she wasn't asked. And she got the job.

Something similar happened when Liz left the Executive Director position and started a tenure track job as a business law professor. Teaching business law to relatively small classes of undergraduate students requires the following skills: comfort with public speaking, an ability to improvise, an ability to connect with an audience and gain their respect and trust, and the capacity to translate complex legal ideas into relatively simple terms. It also requires the creativity to come up with engaging materials and comprehensive assignments.

Former litigators tend to make good undergraduate law professors because they already have a lot of these skills. Arguing motions in open court requires the same level of public speaking ability as teaching in a classroom. Responding to questions from a judge requires the same ability to improvise. Persuading a jury requires the same ability to connect with an audience and gain their respect and trust. Advising clients about their legal options requires the same ability to translate legal concepts into everyday language. Moving from litigation to academia requires a big shift in the environment you work in, but the skill sets that are necessary for success are much the same.

The substance, however, is not necessarily the same, even in teaching law. In the first course she taught, one of the subjects was securities regulation. Liz did not understand securities law at all. She had never studied it in law school, never encountered it on a bar exam, and truly had no interest in the subject at all (and still doesn't). Because it was a required part of the course, however, she had to learn it. The general research and study skills that got you through your J.D. are more than enough to help you learn about something new.

You can learn new substantive material more easily than you can develop a new skill. If you can make it through law school, you can read a book about angel investing or any other field you want to go into. If the new substantive material you are learning is something you have little interest in, or which bores you to tears, that's probably a sign that you are considering the wrong field. Skills, along with character, are the hardest things to develop: and **you have already developed them**. You just need to demonstrate that to a non-legal employer by demonstrating the equivalence.

In practice, the best way to do that is to revise your CV thoroughly, paying special attention to what you have done in each of your positions and rephrasing them in more general terms. In almost every area of law, lawyers develop common skills and abilities that are tremendously valuable outside the legal field. The fact that we use so much legalese to describe them makes it harder for other people to recognize their more general value. Once we take the legal substance out of our experiences, in review, the objective value of our skills should become much clearer.

Reframing Skills for Career Leverage

According to the World Economic Forum, technological innovation is going to lead to a substantial shift in the skills necessary to succeed in the business world in the coming decades. Its 2020

Future of Jobs Report provided a list of what the most valuable professional skills are likely to be in 2025.[104] These include:

1. Problem solving skills, including analytical thinking and innovation, complex problem solving, critical thinking and analysis, reasoning and ideation, and creativity, originality and initiative

2. Self-management skills, including active learning, resilience, stress tolerance, and flexibility

3. Working with people skills, including leadership and social influence

If you're thinking, "I have these skills," you're almost certainly right. But how do you show off these skills when they are camouflaged in the law-specific descriptions of work that are likely to be on your CV right now? How do you develop the ability to showcase these skills while you are networking with people who view you as "just" a lawyer? These are some of the most important issues that all lawyers have to confront when they are considering a career change.

No matter what path you have taken in law school and beyond it, there are ways to reframe and repurpose the skills you have developed. By looking more closely at what you have done as a lawyer, and taking the legal substance out of it, you will be able to see a much broader range of opportunities to use those skills. For the purpose of this next section, think about the elements of your past legal experience and how they might be reframed according to the categories below.

1. Legal Research = Research, Analytical Thinking, Written Communication Skills

From the first weeks of law school, when students start reading and explaining cases, lawyers develop the ability to understand case law. Finding out what the case law suggests about the likely resolution of any particular fact pattern sends lawyers to online legal databases like Westlaw and Lexis to research relevant decisions in the appropriate jurisdiction. Whether you are writing a research memorandum, a brief, or any other kind of legal document relating to litigation, it is critical to understand "what the law says" and which cases best support your argument.

The ability to do that kind of legal research is comparable to other kinds of research. The critical review and evaluation of information, in general, is a useful skill in other contexts. Lawyers are accustomed to using cases, with occasional reference to compilations and other guides, as the authority for their arguments in court. But the same kind of critical analysis and marshalling of information is used in every other kind of research. The "legal" in "legal research" becomes auxiliary when you look at the value of that core skill in the marketplace.

Another skill that lawyers use in doing legal research is issue spotting. At the earliest stages of a legal matter, lawyers look at the situation before them and identify the potential legal issues. There is a good reason that issue spotting exams are such a common part of law school course assessment. Because problems in the real world do not come with law-related labels, an essential part of a lawyer's skill set is the ability to match potentially troubling fact patterns to the most appropriate areas of law and the most relevant laws in that area.

These issue spotting skills are highly transferable. Issue spotting in the business world is comparable to risk management. Both involve identifying potential sources of legal or financial risk and proposing solutions to help mitigate those risks.

2. Depositions = Analytical Thinking, Interpersonal Communication, Attention to Detail

Whether you are taking a deposition or defending a deposition, you are using generally applicable skills in the context of a discovery process that few people outside of law practice know or care about. The process itself, however, reveals how useful these skills can be in other contexts.

Preparing to take a deposition involves several different talents. The first is analysis, because you cannot establish your goals for the deposition without being able to analyze the factual information as well as the legal consequences of what a witness might say or not say. How will you know if you have conducted a successful deposition if you don't know the information you need to get from that particular witness? Forming good deposition questions involves writing and editing skills, so that your questions do not raise objections as to their form. While few non-lawyers care about whether a question is objectionable per se, the value of being able to craft careful language is a widely valued skill.

Once you have formed the questions, the skill of listening closely to the witness and following up on any additional material she introduces is valuable in itself. This skill of careful listening requires a deposing lawyer to be sensitive, attentive, and flexible. Most litigators have seen depositions in which the questioning lawyer fails to hear or follow up on something the deponent says that could lead to some especially valuable or juicy information. An excellent listener will know the right way to follow up when a deponent leaves a possibility open or offers only a partial answer.

Defending a deposition also requires the skill of careful listening. The defending lawyer is the most important protection a client has to an objectionable question. For that reason, the defending lawyer has to be on her guard throughout the deposition, making sure that everything her client is asked is in accord with the procedural rules.

The defending lawyer is also more likely to be successful if she has good interpersonal communication skills. Preparing a witness to be deposed can be a delicate process, and one that requires paying close attention to what the witness is likely to say to the questions the lawyer can anticipate. Witnesses who feel well prepared for their depositions have usually worked closely with at least one lawyer in advance. The better that lawyer is at interpersonal communication, the better their witness will do under oath at the deposition.

3. Representing = Advising, Counseling, Liaising

Getting to actually meet your clients is an experience that not all lawyers, especially associates in Big Law firms, have on a regular basis. But the experience of meeting with clients, understanding their concerns, explaining their legal options and alternatives, and representing their interests encompasses a number of skills that are valuable outside of the context of legal representation. As with taking depositions, counseling a client requires a lawyer to be an excellent listener. If you cannot understand a client's objectives, you are not likely to be able to help meet them.

Whether you have a large corporate client, represented by any number of in-house counsel, or a smaller client whom you represent more directly, all client relations boil down to person-to-person communications. The client has to be able to trust you, and you have to be able to trust that the client is giving you all the information you ask for. If you have enjoyed the challenge of representing a client, you have probably developed stellar inter-personal communication skills. Knowing what to say and when and how to say it is an invaluable part of effective client representation.

But client representation is about more than just great inter-personal communication. Another critical but perhaps less obvious skill is translation. Translation is the ability to take a complicated set of cases, facts, witnesses, and other considerations that affect the outcome of a lawsuit and turn them into a set of options and suggestions that the client can understand fairly well. This is especially true when your clients are not lawyers themselves. Non-lawyers need to understand the impact of their litigation options in terms of the impact on their businesses or their lives. A great trusted advisor has developed the skill of translating the babble of litigation into options a more general audience can understand.

4. Arguing = Advocacy, Originality, Creative Problem Solving

The ability to make a cogent argument is a hallmark legal skill. In fact, making arguments in court is one of the most rewarding aspects of litigation for many courtroom lawyers. One of the more frustrating aspects of Big Law associate life is that the opportunity to make those arguments does not come along as often as we might want it to. Whether we make arguments in writing, in court, or in the course of any kind of negotiation, the ability to make an effective argument is an important outcome of a lot of legal training and experience. The ability to serve as an advocate allows us to add weight to our client's side of the scales of justice.

The advocate's ability to make an argument can translate into the general skill of persuasion, including being able to change the minds of decision makers. In many businesses, the people who need to be persuaded of a particular proposition could include upper-level management, the Board of Directors, or another group of executives with significant decision-making power. Someone who has demonstrated the ability to win a motion or a case has also demonstrated the ability to make a persuasive argument in a boardroom or an online meeting.

Because of the adversarial nature of law, making arguments effectively also requires a certain amount of creative thinking. How will we deal with the opposing side's counter-arguments? It is usually important to anticipate the other side's best arguments and figure out how best to overcome them. In the context of a lawsuit, this might involve addressing case law that is bad for your side, a witness whose testimony hurts your case, or facts that you wish were just slightly different. In a business setting, the same dynamic might involve anticipating the objections to your proposal, addressing the "cons" to your "pros," and marshaling the statistics and market research that support your views. The skill set is the same, although the specific elements of the argument are certainly different.

5. Case management = Leadership, Project Management, Logistics, Analysis

In order to manage a case, a lawyer needs to have a broad sense of many different moving parts. There are the pleadings to consider, arguments to develop, legal research underlying and supporting those arguments. There is discovery to manage, both in terms of the discovery requests the firm proposes to make on behalf of a client, and the responses to incoming discovery requests that the client needs to be corralled to provide. There are motions to make, communication with the client to maintain, and a host of other complex considerations. There is also a team of lawyers and paralegals to manage, and, ideally, to keep informed and engaged. If you have ever managed a case, you have project management skills. Although we do not generally use the phrase "project management" in that context, that is exactly what it is.

To be clear, we are not suggesting that you lie when you reframe your legal experience for the purposes of a non-legal career. We think it is critical to recharacterize your experience in terms that anyone can understand. Despite all the TV shows and movies about lawyers and the justice system, the reality of what lawyers do day to day is a black box for most people. That is not unique to law; it's true for almost every career. So it is incumbent on us to explain, truthfully and carefully, how the skills we have developed in various aspects of our legal careers are relevant outside of that black box. Decoupling the substance from the skills we have acquired is a form of education, not misrepresentation.

Learning how to reframe your legal experience in terms that any non-lawyer can understand is a critical step toward exploring your non-legal career options. It is your responsibility to show what you can do for an employer. The more you can highlight the value of your skills outside of the legal context you developed them in, the better. It is unrealistic to expect people outside of the legal field to understand how to evaluate your legal experience on their own. There may be some employers who don't have to be convinced of the value of hiring lawyers for non-legal positions. A friend of ours had the wonderful luck to apply for a job where the person evaluating candidates was married to a former lawyer, and therefore understood how fungible our skills can be. Most employers, however, need to be shown how your legal experience translates into the development of skills they can use.

CHAPTER 9

Networking to Reconnect in a Post-COVID World

*"You will sometimes go against the grain to build relationships,
increase goodwill, and make decisions based on what's better
for the business long-term and your reputation.
Don't be afraid to embrace it."*[105]

—Wendi Weiner, lawyer and founder of The Writing Guru

Suing Your Alma Mater? Not As Outlandish As It Sounds

IN 2009, TRINA THOMPSON of the Bronx made headlines for bringing a lawsuit against her alma mater, New York's Monroe College,[106] to try to recoup the $70,000 she paid in tuition to secure a degree in Informational Technology. Thompson graduated in the spring of 2008, and by August of that same year, when she didn't yet have a job, she filed a *pro se* claim, alleging that the Office of Career Advancement failed to help her get a job. In the pleadings, she took issue with the fact that the "Office of Career Advancement Information Technology Counselor did not make sure their e-recruiting clients call the graduates that recently finished college for a [sic] interview to get a job placement. They have not tried hard enough to help me."[107]

While there is no publicly available disposition to the case, most commentators agreed at the time, and since, that the lawsuit had dubious merit. Monroe College made an immediate statement denouncing the lawsuit, and told the New York Times in 2009 that it was still willing to help Thompson as the Office of Career Advancement offers its alum counseling services for life.[108]

Thompson's case is often included in lists of frivolous and ridiculous lawsuits, and while we don't pretend to know enough about Thompson's actual case facts from the limited pleadings available, we are struck by an inherent truth in her so-called outlandish claim: that networking can indeed land you a job. At its core, her complaint alleges that if the right people at the right time connected her to the right source, jobs could be had. Careers could be built. Dreams could be made. And you know what? Thompson was right about that.

The Career Advancement offices of your various schools, from high school to law school, may well provide solid leads for networking your future career path. Ask that of them. Show up. Make appointments. Follow up on their leads. Ms. Thompson was right. That office should work for you and help you make the most of your degree.

But here's where we disagree with Ms. Thompson. Leaving that kind of connection-making entirely to others misses the mark. You'll need to be proactive in building and creating organic connections. Also, Ms. Thompson's speedy lawsuit a few months after graduation demonstrates a lack of patience and persistence, which are necessary ingredients in the job search: both the first time around … and every time after that. It takes a while to meet people, form authentic connections, and garner enough trust and good will to make meaningful asks.

In a post-Covid world, less patient job seekers will be relieved to know that many relevant connections can and will be made online, potentially shortening the timelines from what they were even a year or two ago. We will explore more about that below. But be careful to cultivate relationships that can stand on their own in the real live world. We will explore more about that below as well.

LinkedIn 101

How to get started? Well, because we know all of this can feel a bit overwhelming, we want to remind you that baby steps really are the best way forward. Small, manageable tasks will help propel you forward without inviting the kind of overwhelm that paralyzes many would-be transitioning lawyers. To that end, when looking to connect in the post-Covid world, it's still best to rely on some of the ways you connected in the pre-Covid world as well. For example, if you've already got a LinkedIn account, then you've got a great tool in your arsenal to start networking for a life after law right away. And if not, setting up a LinkedIn account is as easy as entering your name and a password. (No, really. Apparently every second, two new professionals sign up for LinkedIn. *That's* how easy it is.)[109]

Importantly, whether you already have a LinkedIn page set up or not, you should spend a little time thinking about the best practices for that page.[110] Here are some easy steps for maximizing its use as you think about transitioning from your law gig: make sure your profile is up to date and thoroughly detailed, be a *joiner*, and for extra credit *blog*.

Make sure your profile is thoroughly detailed: Now is not the time to edit or omit. Include your law school, college, high school, grade school, every gig you ever had (summers, too!), every company you ever worked for, and all the volunteer positions and board memberships you've had over the years. Now is the time to expand your circle, not circumscribe it. By giving lots of people a potential point of connection with you, you can maximize your presence on this powerful platform. You just never know whether someone from the graduating class of your middle school years is doing something really incredible with their law degree and is dying to tell you all about it, until you make yourself easy to be found!

Be a Joiner. An easy way to expand your network is to join LinkedIn Groups. Search for groups by geography, trade, alumni associations, relevant hobbies, and other points of connection. And while we're on this topic, this is a good time to remind you that while the LinkedIn mobile App is a perfectly acceptable way to use LinkedIn, you will still gain the most by using LinkedIn's desktop version. For comprehensive searches of potential groups and more, we recommend using the desktop version of LinkedIn to make and search connections, to search and create groups. The mobile app is great, too, but more so for reading content on the go, liking and commenting to create initial connections and build your circle of like-minded connections. (Also! Could we be so bold as to recommend you join the *How to Leave the Law* LinkedIn Group? Great! See you there.)

For extra credit, *blog*. LinkedIn's blogging platform, Pulse, previously a separate platform, is now fully integrated into the LinkedIn platform. When you scroll through the feed, you will gain access to new articles from influencers and connections you follow. A great way to make new connections is by adding to that content yourself. Navigate to your home page, and click on "Write an Article" to get started.

Of course, once you start making potential connections, you're going to want to actually *connect* with them. You can start this process on the LinkedIn platform by direct messaging folks you meet there. But it will soon become useful to go beyond that platform for more meaningful conversations.

What's next? Glad you asked! (Spoiler alert: you'll have more options than we did a decade ago).

When Zoom Became the BOMB

While we didn't have Zoom when we were transitioning from the law (cue the "when we were younger, we walked uphill both ways in the snow" anecdotes here), Zoom was already a large player in the virtual meeting space even before Covid. There can be little doubt that Zoom makes the informational meetings and coffee dates of the past much easier to plan and execute; it also creates access to potential contacts that might previously have been out of geographic range.

Launched in 2013, Zoom had 400,000 people sign up within the first month. By the end of its first year of operations, Zoom reported 200 million meeting minutes.[111] Then in 2020, not surprisingly, the Zoom Mobile app was downloaded 485 million times, boasting 300 million daily use participants (up from 10 million in 2019) and increasing the annual meeting minutes figure to 3.3 trillion.[112]

This incredible growth of Zoom included pains, of course, with a new concept being added to the virtual meeting lexicon: "zoombombing." In 2021, Zoom agreed to settle a pending class action suit alleging insufficient privacy measures by Zoom had led to a widespread hacking phenomenon wherein "strangers" found their way into private meetings and disrupted them, sometimes simply as a nuisance, and sometimes with more violent and disturbing results.[113]

While many believe that Zoombombing occurs largely when outsiders troll for unsuspecting groups to harass, a research group out of Boston University actually concluded that the most common way would-be Zoombombers get their access to meeting spaces is through meeting insiders,[114] making enhancement of security of virtual meeting spaces inherently complicated.

The finding from the Boston University researchers also begs the question: why are so many insiders helping sabotage their virtual meeting spaces? Consider the "online disinhibition effect": one explanation for Zoombombing that also makes online networking more complicated than it appears at first glance.[115]

In 2004, John Suler, professor of psychology at Rider University, published an article titled "The Online Disinhibition Effect," which sought to explain a phenomenon that was being discussed in many circles at the time. For Suler, online disinhibition could be either "benign" or "toxic" including behavior in which people in the virtual space might be more kind, less buttoned up, and more eager to connect with and help others because of various psychological factors. On the other hand, Suler said, those same psychological factors could lead to more rudeness and even dangerous behaviors like pornography, crime, and harassment.

The six psychological factors identified by Suler are relevant in a discussion of what works and what doesn't in the world of online networking. They are:

Dissociative anonymity: Of course, sometimes we feel more anonymous than we actually are, but still, communicating with someone you've never met, and will likely never meet in real person can lead to a freedom which can in turn lead to benign or toxic effects.

Invisibility: Is your camera off? Literally or figuratively? When we are communicating as part of a larger group, or in any other way that includes only text and no visual contact, Suler argues that the lack of visible body cues might lead to inhibitions being lowered; again with mixed results.

Asynchronicity: Suler says the asynchronous nature of many forms of communication over the internet leads to disinhibition. Sometimes this results in more impassioned, spontaneous (even thoughtless) communication, while at other times, it leads to more thoughtful, carefully planned communications than might otherwise be had at an "in real life" meeting.

Solipsistic Introjection: This is a fancy way of saying that your online contacts can start to take on characteristics in your mind that they don't have in real life. We may even assign to them characteristics that remind us of, well, our own selves, which can lead to a perception that we are actually talking to ourselves. There's a comfort in solipsistic introjection, then, that can lead to disinhibition, both benign and toxic.

Dissociative Imagination: Suler thinks we sometimes treat this whole online interaction thing as a "game" of sorts, trying out different personas and reinventing ourselves in the context of a new interaction. This can be very helpful and positive in auditioning for a life after law, but without authentic connection, you might be missing the mark of online networking.

Minimization of Status and Authority: You might feel less intimidated and more of an "even playing field" via online interactions, a fact that could actually help maximize online meeting productivity. Certainly all of these factors can combine to make online networking more productive and efficient, but as Suler's research shows (and as indicated by the emergence of Zoombombing instigated by "inside" sources in recent years), online disinhibition can have toxic effects as well.[116]

Instead, we want to advocate for Zoom, LinkedIn, and other similar digital platforms (with proper safety protocols in place) to be used and supplemented with live networking opportunities as discussed herein.

Lessons Learned in the Clubhouse

In April 2020, just as the world was shutting down, a new social media networking app was launching called Clubhouse.[117] Leveraging its perfect launch timing with a faux exclusivity (for the first year or so of its existence, you could only log in with an invite from an existing member), Clubhouse became a sort of cult phenomenon reaching 10 million users by February 2021, less than a year into its launch.[118] Elon Musk, Mark Zuckerberg, Tiffany Haddish, Drake, and Oprah were among the celebrities vouching for Clubhouse by joining in the discussions, and the app seemed poised for an impressive growth trajectory in its second year of existence.

But then it went away. By the fall of 2021, Clubhouse had diminished in popularity, with fewer and fewer references in the Twitterverse and other social media apps, and with dramatically decreasing numbers of downloads and users as 2021 came to a close.[119]

What happened? The more relevant question is probably what didn't happen. Clubhouse boasts an intimacy and casual atmosphere made possible through audio-only participation, and user forums that are dominated by speakers who do all the speaking. A so-called networking app that exists without any eye contact, visual cues, or importantly, any real engagement, Clubhouse became all but obsolete as the world started to reopen for real live events and networking opportunities. It seems that those who predicted that Covid would forever change the way we network, replacing live networking entirely with virtual and digital networking methods, turned out to be wrong. Mostly. And we are seeing the hybrid use of virtual and live networking forums emerging post-Covid.

So, in light of what we know about online disinhibition, Suler's research, and the real-life example of Clubhouse's rise and fall, what will be required going forward? A new and improved social networking app? Some other new tricks?

We'd argue instead for more of the old tricks. Like empathy, authenticity, and diversity just to name a few. Wait a minute. Does it sound like we've entered a therapy session instead of a how-to guide? Well, let's pause for a moment to understand why.

An Impromptu Counselor Counseling Session

While Covid expanded the realm of online networking, and made it a more viable option than ever before, psychotherapists argue that it's unlikely Covid and its resulting aftermath will ever truly obviate the need for connection or in-person networking. In fact, quite the opposite.

As Esther Perel, renowned therapist and New York Times bestseller says, disaster actually accelerates the need for relationship and connection. The accompanying fear of mortality and feelings of loss lead us to reach out and yearn for personal, live connection.[120] Of course, post-Covid, our need to connect is complicated by the fact that this particular preceding disaster was caused by contact itself that was dangerous and life-threatening. We want to connect. But connection nearly killed us off. As a result we find ourselves in a kind of bizarre spiral of need and fear surrounding live interactions.

Take the example of news reporters interviewed by Perel in 2021.[121] The journalists of a large media source gathered to discuss feelings of overwhelm. They reported that the lack of collaboration, the lack of actual "face time" and crippling isolation had wreaked havoc on their emotional states.[122] Also affected were the journalists' relationships at home, with family and partners. The fact that only one or a few persons had been asked to bear the burden of all the missing in-person interactions had in turn burdened the relationships at home as well.[123]

As Perel notes, during the global lockdown, we were "not working from home. We were working with home." Perel argues there has never, in modern times, been such a collapse of boundaries. People who had never even come over to our homes for dinner were now invited into our bedrooms for zoom calls and virtual work meetings. This breakdown of boundaries and barriers, the elimination of commutes, changing of clothes, changing of environments from one audience to another, created mental and emotional confusion, Perel says.

It follows then, that to continue networking in only virtual spaces (without changing clothes, commutes, attitudes) is not the best course of action for all of us—emotionally, physically, and mentally—in the post-Covid world. Put simply, just because we now *can*, doesn't mean we *should*.

Perel cautions that it's important to create rituals and boundaries that will support and reinforce our interpersonal relationships. And it's important to strengthen the structure that will reinforce the rituals.[124] That's not to say we completely abandon our virtual networking devices. It's just that we have to reconcile the fact that these devices which we previously thought, pre-Covid, would completely eliminate connection in the extreme, when put to the test became our only viable form of connection.[125]

One way to make virtual networking a more productive endeavor [and thus gain the benign (i.e., positive)] benefits of online disinhibition) is to use it to create empathetic relationships. Take time, regardless of whether you are meeting with someone live or online, to ask more relational questions like these:

• Are you taking care of any additional people?
• Who is taking care of you?
• Have you lost anyone?
• Do you have a pet?
• Have you attended any events in person lately?

Experts agree that empathy is both a requirement and a challenge of networking post-Covid. "While the challenges of networking across time zones remain, bringing an empathetic approach to networking is key to bridging the digital divide," according to Professor Gregory Whitwell, Dean of the University of Sydney School of Business.[126] And in her book, *Reclaiming Conversation,* Sherry Turkle, the Abby Rockefeller Mauze Professor of Social Studies of Science and Technology at MIT, advocated that we be wary of the ease of networking via technology, as its widespread use can have other implications; she also suggested that "technology is implicated in an assault on empathy."[127]

Another important aspect of post-Covid networking is authenticity. And reclaiming authenticity may require reconnecting with and networking with someone very important. Yourself. Sound strange? Well, consider Turkle's argument that "[s]olitude is where we learn to trust our imaginations ... This is the space where creativity arises." So let yourself be alone, too.[128]

Stated another way, authenticity can actually be undermined by *over-networking*. In a post-Covid world, where many of us feel deprived of in-person social contact, over-networking is both a temptation and a hazard.

Another important part of maintaining authenticity in your networking is generosity. As lawyer-turned-fitness guru Robin Arzon says: "Do your research, and evaluate your skill set. Be honest with yourself on what skills you can leverage and what you still need to learn. Tell everyone about your big dream and plant all the seeds but make sure to reciprocate the help. If someone is willing to give their time and advice, you need to offer to be of service in any way you can."[129] You must view networking, not as a sales transaction, where you are buying and selling a commodity, but rather as an on-going research session, in which you are learning. About professions. About other people. About yourself.

Another important post-Covid means of networking that should actually be familiar from the pre-Covid days is cultivating diversity. It's not enough to keep talking to people who are exactly like you or exactly in your same personal and/or professional situation. The only way to broaden your perspective and learn about opportunities you don't even know about yet is to talk to people who are not like you. While this might mean talking to non-lawyers, and those not similarly situated professionally, it will also include diversifying your contacts based on racial, cultural, and geographic differences, in order to cultivate empathy and expand your experience base as you get ready for the next potential leg of your journey.

The bottom line is that we are excited about the opportunities available to you that were not available to us as we were transitioning even a short decade ago. We want you to use and enjoy these new and creative ways to network, and even enjoy the shortened timeline they might provide for those of us (like Ms. Trina Thompson!) who are not so patient. Simultaneously, however, we want to be cautious about you relying exclusively on online networking without any goals of engaging in real life.

People Who Need People

In addition to considering *how* to connect with people in a post-Covid world, it's important to consider *who* to connect with as well. We've read various lists of the kinds of people recommended for your networking lists from sources including *Medium* to *Forbes*. Lists that have included everyone from a coach, to a mentor, to a cheerleader, to your resident "in the know" workplace know-it-all.[130]

Our advice is to focus on the following three kinds of people in your networking plan.

1. Former lawyers working in a variety of new professions;

2. Former or currently practicing lawyers who are now working also as legal recruiters or transitioning coaches; and

3. Executives who have worked with or hired former lawyers.

If you think that's a lot of lawyers or people connected to lawyers, you're absolutely right. Why, when you are trying to leave the profession, do we recommend that you stay connected to so many different kinds of lawyers? Easy. If you are serious about leaving the law, you will find that there is a community of former lawyers waiting to welcome you to the other side. In fact, there is a unique and particular enthusiasm among transitioning lawyers to welcome you to the other side.

For one thing, your interest, and ultimately, your success, helps validate their decision. You will also be pleased to know that transitioning lawyers generally reside in such a place of great joy that it's hard for them not to want to share the bounty with others.

One of the greatest untapped sources, we believe, of potential networking sources for would-be transitioning lawyers is your local bar association and the ABA as a whole. Many states have dormant or small Lawyers in Transition committees that have historically been reserved only for lawyers who are retiring. But some states have reengineered these committees to be vehicles for change and innovation for the future. Two prime examples are the New Jersey Bar Association and the City of New York Bar Association, both of which have had robust programming in recent years for lawyers interested in a life after law. Does your local city or state bar association have an active Lawyers in Transition Committee? (And if not, think about reinvigorating it, through LinkedIn groups, for starters).

Other opportunities for live engagement can be found through volunteer efforts (or even joining the Boards) for various community organizations that can potentially generate an inside look at various industries you might not otherwise know much about or have in-person connections with. You might also look at the website of your local Chamber of Commerce. What events are available to newcomers such as yourself?

As we get back to the world of conferences and live retreats, think about attending a wellness retreat or other special interest conference that appeals to you. One of our favorite conferences is hosted by iRelaunch, an organization co-founded by the inimitable Carol Fishman Cohen, who helps professionals relaunch their careers after a hiatus. Transitioning lawyers certainly fit this profile, and Cohen welcomes large numbers of lawyers to the iRelaunch conferences, which are held in various cities across the country each year.[131]

And One More Thing ... Here's What Not to Do

We understand that we don't need to counsel you on questions to ask and ways to engage with potential connections. You are lawyers. You ask questions for a living. And there are literally limitless questions you can ask potential connections once you make contact. Always end each meeting or interaction with an authentic "ask" that feels comfortable by the end of the meeting: whether it be to keep in touch or make an introduction to another transitioning attorney.

But we do think it's worth noting a few questions you should *not ask*. At least not right away.

Don't ask them to get your resume to the right place for you (unless you really know them well).

Don't ask them questions about themselves or the company that would be readily available online. (Be sure to do your homework!)

Don't ask open-ended questions, like "Can I pick your brain?" Show some respect for your contact's time. Ask pointed, interested questions instead.

Don't ask whether you should leave your current position. (And by all means, don't speak badly about anyone at your current firm/position! The world is small, especially the legal world).

And last but not least, *don't* ask them if they regret leaving the law ... unless you're prepared for some hearty laughter!

CHAPTER 10

Leaving a Law Firm for Alternative JD-Preferred Careers

"There will be people who say to you, 'you are out of your lane.'
They are burdened by only having the capacity to see
what has always been instead of what can be.
But don't you let that burden you."[132]

—Kamala Harris, former lawyer, Vice President of the United States

WHEN MOST LAWYERS THINK about changing careers, they think about what makes the most sense for someone with a JD. "What can you do with a law degree" and "former lawyer" are the kinds of internet searches they are likely to run. Given all the time and money that we all put into law school and our legal careers, no matter how long or successful they have been, it is easy to understand why one of the first things we might think about is what other careers make for the most seamless transitions. Are there new and more rewarding ways for us to use the substantive knowledge we have? Are there less painful ways to make a real contribution to society without having to bill our time?

Many successful former lawyers have chosen to leave their more traditional law career for another path that is "law-adjacent." Pursuing a law-adjacent career is one of the best ways to use your professional skills to promote justice and to make the world a better place, which is one of the most common reasons people go to law school in the first place. Some former lawyers, like Liz, go on to be law professors in a law school, college, or graduate business programs. Others leverage their expertise in public policy to be advisors to or leaders of nonprofits. Some of the most impactful advocates for change are writers who base their work in part on what they learned in practice. And then there are lawyers who move over to legal tech, starting and running the kinds of innovative companies that help keep law firms competitive. In this chapter, we'll look at specific examples of each of these kinds of transitions.

From Law to Legal Academia

Although most lawyers have only learned law in law school, there are several options for lawyers who want to teach something related to law. In addition to the traditional law school teaching route, there are options to teach clinical practice within law schools. There are also ways to teach legal research and writing without teaching substantive law courses. And there are very rewarding paths open to lawyers teaching legal studies in undergraduate and graduate business programs.

Not all law faculty are tenured. In order to get tenure, you have to apply for a position that is designated as "tenure track." Those positions require a faculty member to develop a track record that combines teaching and scholarship, usually with an emphasis on scholarship, for between five and seven years before the school conducts a tenure review. If the tenure track professor does not get tenure at that point, she is typically given a final teaching term and then asked to leave. If the tenure track professor does get tenure, she can only be fired "for cause," which each school defines differently.

Another category of faculty is the lecturer. Lecturers are not eligible for tenure and have either annual employment contracts or multi-year contracts. In most cases, lecturers focus most of their attention on teaching and spend little, if any, time on scholarship. They tend to have higher teaching loads, meaning that they are obligated to teach more courses over the course of the academic year than tenure track or tenured professors. Although lecturers do not have the same kind of job security as tenured professors, many lecturers prefer their positions because what they really love to do is teaching. A lecturer will spend most of her day preparing for and teaching classes and interacting with students outside of class.

In addition to tenure track/tenured faculty and lecturers, most universities hire adjunct professors to teach some of their classes. Adjuncts are hired to teach course by course rather than year by year. In some schools, adjuncts are unionized, which helps to limit the amount of course development and overload teaching that they are allowed to do. Department chairs usually hire adjuncts to teach specific courses and often have a roster of adjuncts that they call on regularly.

If you have never taught before, we recommend teaching at least a course or two as an adjunct before you decide whether to pursue a full-time teaching gig. The benefits of teaching as an adjunct are that you get firsthand experience in the classroom. While you may think that you would like teaching, and that teaching is a natural extension of your public speaking and oral advocacy skills, there is no substitute for the experience of running a classroom in real life. Teaching as an adjunct allows you to try on the role of law school faculty while making practically no long-term commitment to the field. There are, of course, downsides to teaching as an adjunct. First, you make virtually no money doing it. Second, it takes a lot of time to prepare to teach a course. Not only do you have to figure out the best way to deliver the material, but you also have to develop ways to assess your students' learning. That is, you have to create tests and/or paper assignments that you then have to grade. Next, you have to deal with the students who are unhappy with their grades. Finally, adjuncts have little to no control over their teaching schedule. By the time an adjunct is hired, the days and times in which the course is taught have usually been fixed by the university. These class times are often compatible with many working schedules, however, since the expectation is that an adjunct will have at least one other job that provides a livable wage.

Teaching, Scholarship and Service

Law faculty are hired on the basis of their teaching skills and/or scholarship. The relative importance of teaching and scholarship will depend not only on the particular position a faculty member is being hired for, but also on the school itself. Teaching skills can come from experience actually teaching in classes, but they can also stem from some aspects of law practice. Arguing a motion in court requires a litigator to be adept at explaining things to a less familiar audience. Delivering an opening or closing argument uses the same skills. In some cases, a school may be willing to bet that a faculty candidate will be a skilled teacher based in part on court-room experience.

Scholarship refers to a track record of publishing long, foot-note-heavy articles on some aspect of the law in a law review or business law journal. Not all journals are considered equivalent. Just as universities are ranked by outside sources like USA Today, law journals also have a hierarchy of prestige. Journals are ranked by Washington and Lee, according to their influence and the extent to which they are cited in other articles and in judicial opinions. A law professor who has to do some amount of scholarship needs to publish in one of these journals. Some universities have a closed list of the journals in which they will accept or count their faculty's publications. Law professors sometimes write these articles alone and sometimes co-author them with one or two other professors. Author groups of more than three people are relatively rare in law journals. Scholarship can also include publishing a chapter in a scholarly book. When a candidate applies for a teaching position, especially one that is tenure track, they are usually asked to provide not only evidence of their scholarship but also a research agenda that outlines the specific scholarly topics that they are most interested in studying in the years ahead.

If your interest in teaching just screeched to a halt, you are not alone. Developing scholarship is often the most difficult part of the transition from law practice to academia. Scholarship requires thinking deeply and originally about a particular focused issue. If you have been working as a lawyer in a field that you don't particularly like thinking about, you may not want to focus more of your intellectual attention on that field even if it is something that you know well.

But developing scholarship can be an amazing opportunity to learn, think, and write more about something in the world of law that you do find interesting, even if it is not related to your professional experience. The best way to write a scholarly article is to look at some aspect of law that you want to think about in more depth, read what other people have written about that subject in law reviews and other journals, and then find something unique to say about that subject. Once you write your scholarly article, you need to persuade law review editors to publish your work. They are most likely to do so if you can persuade them that your article adds something new and valuable to the existing conversation among scholars on that subject. Conversely, law reviews are not likely to accept an article that rehashes or simply repeats the points that other scholars have already made.

Once hired, law faculty may also be expected to provide some amount of service as well. Service can include things like serving on committees within the school. These committees could focus on curriculum development and implementation, hiring, faculty governance, or any of a number of other operational issues that all schools face. Service might also take the form of advising a student group or managing a department within the school. In some cases, faculty members move up from teaching to administration, meaning that they choose to focus on operational administration rather than teaching classes directly. Former lawyers who apply for faculty positions may be evaluated in part on their ability to perform these kinds of service, but service is rarely the primary consideration for filling an open faculty position.

Law School Faculty

Most law school faculty focus on teaching substantive courses to law students. In order to become a tenure-track law school faculty member, there are certain requirements common to most law schools. It helps to have graduated from a top law school yourself. It helps to have done scholarly research, usually in the form of writing lengthy articles that are published in law reviews edited by law students. In many cases, it helps to have some experience teaching. This tends to be less important at the initial stages of law school faculty hiring because there is some recognition that it is hard to get teaching experience before you become a professor.

Legal Research and Writing Instructors

A second category of law school faculty is Legal Research and Writing (LRW) instructors. As you would expect, these faculty members teach students how to write like lawyers. They can also teach students how to do legal research, interview clients, and construct the bases for oral arguments. LRW faculty may be charged with running moot court programs as well. In some law schools, LRW faculty can be tenure track or tenured. In other law schools, LRW faculty are hired as lecturers with annual contracts, having less job security.

Clinical Faculty

Law schools also hire clinical faculty to teach law students professional skills and to supervise assistance with clients. Clinical faculty can include the directors who run clinics through which the law school offers (usually) free legal support to clients with specific profiles. These clinics can focus on criminal law, mediation, legal aid, immigration, environmental law, health law, housing law, or supporting veterans. In addition to providing vital assistance for clients, these clinics help students develop skills that will help them become better lawyers. Law students can learn research and writing, advocacy, advisory, and interviewing skills by working in these clinics. While some clinical director positions can lead to tenure, those positions usually require the faculty member to do some amount of scholarship as well in order to earn tenure.

There are other kinds of clinical faculty as well. Externship directors organize the placement of law students into externships and help ensure that they have the skills necessary to be successful in those placements. They are charged with creating new externships and ensuring that there are enough extern positions to meet the demands of the school. These positions are usually but not always filled by people who have JDs themselves, and may or may not be eligible for tenure. The people who advise law students on their coursework and how best to succeed in law school usually are not "faculty" per se, but many schools hire former lawyers into these positions.

Applying for Jobs Teaching Law in Law Schools

The job market for teaching in most accredited law schools has a process all its own. The Association of American Law Schools (AALS) centralizes the hiring process through a collective Faculty Recruitment Service that takes place throughout the fall and early winter every year. Candidates in this centralized process fill out a Faculty Appointments Register (FAR) form that is distributed to the hiring law schools. This form is fairly detailed and provides an overview of each candidate to the schools' hiring committees. Some law schools offer support for alumni who are interested in applying for positions through the AALS. If this interests you, it is worth asking your law school career services office if this is something they can help you with. Many law schools also hire outside of the AALS hiring season, especially when they are filling a position off season.

The basic materials you need when you apply for a law school position are the same whether you use the AALS Faculty Recruitment Service or not. These include not only your CV, but also proof that you have done some scholarship. It is more difficult to apply for a law school faculty position before you have any academic publications under your belt. Candidates also need to submit research agendas, which summarize their research interests.

College or Business School Law Faculty

But law schools are not the only places that hire law professors. We are fairly biased when we say that teaching outside of a law school is much more fun than teaching in a law school because Amy is an adjunct faculty member at Drexel University and Liz is now a tenured law professor at Bentley University and teaches primarily at the college level. One of the great "aha" moments of Liz's career transition happened when a business law professor at Bentley, a university which does not have a law school, took her aside during a community program for working mothers and suggested that she might enjoy teaching law. Liz had absolutely no interest in teaching law students. One of the reasons she wanted to leave law in the first place was to get some distance from the prickly and contentious personalities that seemed so common in her Big Law experience. She also had no interest in teaching the kinds of law courses that she struggled through herself. She had gotten a quarter of the way through a Civil Procedure course without having understood what civil procedure was.

Liz had enjoyed explaining law to her business clients. As the professor pointed out, the college students at Bentley were studying business, and were likely to become the kinds of executives that Big Law firms tend to represent. If advising business leaders was rewarding, could it be as rewarding to teach basic legal concepts to college students? Liz spent three semesters teaching introductory "legal and ethical environment of business" (LEEB) courses to college students as an adjunct professor, earning just a few thousand dollars per course, before applying for a full-time faculty position at the same university where she had been an adjunct.

As in law schools, business law professors fall into three categories: tenured or tenure track, lecturer, and adjunct. Unlike law schools, colleges and business schools only hire directly and there is no central coordination of business law faculty hiring.

Applying for Jobs Teaching Law Outside of Law Schools

If you are looking for a position teaching law in a college or graduate school, there are two critical ways to optimize your search.

1. Join the ALSB

The first is to join the main professional association of law professors who teach outside of law schools: the Academy of Legal Studies in Business (ALSB). Founded in 1924, the ALSB is an international organization with several affiliated regional associations covering various parts of the United States and Canada. Its members teach law in a broad range of institutions, most often in colleges with business programs and in business schools that require some elements of legal education as part of the graduate degree. There are special interest groups within ALSB that focus on areas such as environmental law, employment, technology, sports and entertainment, and teaching and pedagogy. ALSB also offers a mentorship program for new faculty that pairs them with more experienced members of the Academy. A central purpose of the ALSB is to help business law professors become better scholars, teachers, and advocates.

One of the most striking aspects of ALSB is how collegial it is. This can cause a bit of culture shock for people who have become used to the competitive jostling that lawyers often have with each other, especially in gender-diverse professional associations. Although nearly every ALSB member has a law degree, there is a tremendous amount of mutual respect and a pervasive sense of friendliness among the membership. The best way to witness this is to attend its annual meeting, which takes place in late July or early August in a different location every year. At the annual meetings, business law faculty from all over the world give short presentations on the papers they are working on or have already published. There is also a Master Teacher competition, where four professors who have been pre-selected from a competitive field of applicants demonstrate some innovative way to teach a particular business law issue in the classroom. The attendees then vote on the best presentation, and the winner receives an award at a banquet at the end of the meeting. The annual meeting is the best way to make professional connections and learn more about the topics you want to explore as well as the people who focus on them.

There are also annual meetings of the regional associations throughout the year. These often offer people who are new to the idea of legal scholarship a chance to try out presenting their work and to get feedback on their project ideas. It is also an excellent place to meet potential co-authors. Co-authoring with a more experienced faculty member is the best way to learn how to write and place an article successfully in a law review.

ALSB members are among the first to know when there are openings for faculty to teach law outside of law schools. Members usually post their job openings in discussion groups that are open only to ALSB members at the same time they post those openings in general academic publications such as the Chronicle of Higher Education.

2. Develop a Teaching Resume

The biggest mistake you can make in applying for a faculty position is assuming that your professional experience as a lawyer speaks for itself. While many lawyers would like to become academics, only those who make the effort to translate their professional experience into the language of academia are likely to be considered seriously for an open faculty position. As we recommend in Chapters 7 and 8, it is important to tailor your CV and cover letter to the specific job opening you are applying for. In academia, however, it is especially important to do so because so many lawyers overestimate the extent to which their legal work will appeal to hiring chairs. The dangers of this kind of hubris are especially great for lawyers who are coming from an insular world. The fact that a JD is required for almost all law teaching positions doesn't mean that academic employers will perform the kind of extrapolation analysis on a lawyer's CV that the lawyer might expect.

Instead, create a teaching resume. If you have never taught anything before, find any opportunity to lead a class or a training. Is there some kind of advice you can present to junior lawyers at your firm? To other lawyers through your bar association? To people who live in your town through a community education program? The best kind of teaching experience you can show on your CV is having been an adjunct. That will also give you something substantive to talk about in your cover letter and interview, if you can get one. If you have been a litigator, it is also helpful to reframe that experience in terms that will resonate with someone who is looking for an explicit indication of teaching experience. You might create a new section of your CV, for example, that highlights "Public Speaking" and includes references to the motions you have argued in court.

Whether you teach law in a law school, a college, or a graduate business program, academia is one of the most flexible and rewarding ways to leave the legal profession for a law-adjacent role.

From Law to Public Policy

Some lawyers move from legal practice into roles that allow them to make a greater impact on the public policies that concern them the most. Becoming an advocate for causes that matter deeply to them allows them to create more change than they can while working within the systems they want to reform.

One example of a lawyer turned advocate is Jessica Henry. Jessica became interested in criminal law while she was still in college. After studying at New York University School of Law, she worked as a public defender in New York for almost a decade before joining the Department of Justice Studies at Montclair State University as a faculty member. She now focuses her attention on reforming the criminal justice system in which she used to work. Jessica's 2020 book, *Smoke but No Fire: Convicting the Innocent of Crimes that Never Happened*, won the Montaigne Medal award for the "most thought-provoking" book as well as the First Horizon Award for "superior writing" by a "debut author."

From Law to Legal Tech

Other lawyers capitalize on their legal experience to develop and lead companies that innovate in legal technology. There are also many examples of lawyers who use their legal skills to start up companies unrelated to law, and several of these former lawyers are profiled in Chapter 11.

Some lawyers will be threatened by the products Summize offers, which make contract writing and management easier and more streamlined. Others will be thrilled by the idea of a software program that makes contracts simpler to deal with. Summize was founded by its CEO, Tom Dunlop, who is a former general counsel and global legal director for several technology companies. Another example of an innovative lawyer leading a legal tech company is Phil Rosenthal. Phil's path to law school was almost as unusual as his career path after law school. Before attending Harvard Law School, Phil received his doctorate from CalTech in string cosmology. After law school, he worked at Covington & Burling in Washington, D.C. before leaving three years later to start Fastcase, one of the country's leading online legal research software companies. Fastcase merged with its closest competitor, Casemaker, in 2021, continuing operations under the Fastcase name.

From Law to Legal Recruiting

Another law-adjacent field is legal recruiting. Some of the most successful legal recruiters are former lawyers who understand the world of private practice from an insider's perspective. Recruiting allows them to use their analytical skills, understanding of people, and knowledge of law practice to create synergies between candidates and legal roles.

At Major, Lindsey & Africa, one of the world's most prestigious legal executive search firms, Nancy Reiner is a Partner. Nancy is in charge of In-House Counsel Recruiting in the Boston office. Before becoming a recruiter, Nancy spent more than 20 years practicing law at firms, moving from associate to partner at Brown Rudnick as a litigator working on complex commercial and environmental cases. One of her biggest wins was in representing the Commonwealth of Massachusetts in a high stakes case against tobacco manufacturers, resulting in an $8.3 billion settlement for the state.

Recruiting in-house counsel requires a related set of skills and experience. Nancy's litigation career gave her the insights into what corporations need in an in-house counsel. She has led and completed over 100 searches for general counsel, IP counsel, and chief compliance officers in corporate legal departments across the country.

Terri LeComte is another example of a JD who moved into legal recruiting. During law school, she had focused on criminal law, but after getting married it became clear that she could not afford to support a family by working in criminal defense. At the same time, she did not think she would have time to be with her kids if she worked for a large law firm. During her third year of law school, Terri was diagnosed with multiple sclerosis. This solidified her decision not to go into private practice, where she was not sure she would have the energy to do what is usually expected of junior associates. Her experience in the civil litigation clinic during law school, where she sometimes lost sleep worrying about her clients, also confirmed that litigation was not for her.

After getting her JD from Boston University School of Law, Terri worked as its Assistant Director of Admissions. Reading applicants' files and helping to make admission decisions was stressful, but in a more manageable way than being a lawyer would be. Hoping to make more money, Terri left admissions to work in sales, but suffered under a terrible boss until her mother, listening to Terri in tears after another horrible day at work, urged her to quit. And there was more to handle at home. Her first child was born the year after she graduated from law school, followed by a set of triplets four years later.

One of Terri's friends encouraged her to consider legal recruiting because Terri is excellent at talking with people. She first worked with a very small legal recruiting firm. Although the owner trained her well, he wasn't available to provide the opportunities she needed to grow as a recruiter. As an associate at WinterWyman, a general search firm, Terri first worked in the Software Technology practice, and then transitioned to the Executive Search practice before joining FCPG as a Managing Director. In her current role, she has gone back to working with the first legal recruiter who hired her, and who is now in a better position to help her build her career. She specializes in recruiting lawyers for key positions in law firms across the country.

So what makes a good legal recruiter? According to Terri, it is all about building relationships and having a thick skin. Her job, as she sees it, is to find the win-win solutions that match the right candidate with the right law firm. Although most of the candidates she contacts don't return her calls, she listens carefully to the ones who do. She listens for what they are missing, and for the conditions they are looking for in a new firm, and those things don't always emerge right away. The relationships she builds with candidates sometimes result in those same candidates coming back to her a year or two later, when they are looking to move on.

The thick skin is important because the hires don't always come through. Law firms hire other people, and candidates change their minds, sometimes months after the process starts. "This is upsetting the first twelve times it happens," Terri says, but it is all part of the process. The fact that many potential matches fall through is no reason for concern. A recruiter only needs to make a few matches a year in order to do well if she has a good commission arrangement. That said, another factor to consider is that the income from recruiting can be unpredictable, so it may not be the right choice for someone who needs a stable income stream.

If you enjoy talking to people and finding out who they are and what they are looking for, if you want to help lawyers find a better professional match, if you can handle an unpredictable income stream, and if you can let rejection roll off your back, legal recruiting might be worth considering as your next career.

These examples show that there are many ways to leverage your substantive knowledge of law in a wide range of law-adjacent fields. In sum, we understand that leaving the law might mean heading next door rather than leaving the legal world altogether. But if a more drastic change is what you're looking for, read on.

CHAPTER 11

Leaving Law for Non-Law Careers

*"I was passionate about the law but knew
that there was something else."*[133]

—Amanda Jane-Thomas, lawyer turned co-founder of Sip & Sonder

AS WE SAW IN THE LAST CHAPTER, one path out of traditional law practice is to leverage your substantive knowledge of law, the legal world, and law firms in general into a "law-adjacent" career where that kind of expertise is invaluable. Using the content of your legal education and professional experience opens up professional opportunities that are not nearly as accessible for people who have never studied law.

A second career transition path leverages a different kind of strength: the skills you have developed in training to be a lawyer. They might even be the skills that led you to consider law school in the first place. If you grew up winning every argument with your siblings, at some point in your life, we would bet that someone told you, "You should be a lawyer." Although we are going to assume for the moment that they meant well, it is likely that that person meant to compliment you on your logic, your advocacy, your articulateness, your composure under pressure, or some combination of these skills. Lawyers use these strengths to make winning arguments, but there are a hundred other uses for the same skills. The trick is to find a more rewarding use for the skills you have always had, and which you might have honed during law school and beyond.

As we described in Chapter 7, there are four basic steps to finding out what kind of alternative careers are the best fit for you.

The first and most important step in your career transition is to figure out what skills you find most rewarding to use. The second step is figuring out how you want to transfer those skills. Once you have identified what are sometimes called your preferred strengths, you can explore alternative ways to use those strengths in careers that will be more personally satisfying than law. Creating new informal networks is one of the best ways to learn more about alternative careers from the people who are in them now.

The third step is kicking the tires of any potential alternative career. Having identified some alternative options, you can move on to the due diligence phase of career transition: what is it really like to be in the shoes of the person who has what you think of as your ideal job? Is it as great in practice as it sounds in theory? Are the ups and downs of that other career a better fit for your personality and your particular preferences than what you are doing now?

Once you have filtered out the careers that don't capitalize on your preferred strengths and crossed off the careers that sound better on paper than in practice, you can move on to position yourself for success in the career options that remain on your list. This brings us to the fourth step of revising your CV to align more closely with each of your new target careers. The fifth step in the process is capitalizing on your networks to make the kinds of personal connections that uncover job openings before they are posted to the public. These connections also give you an inside edge because they make you less of a risk than a more personally distant candidate.

Learning more about former lawyers who are in a wide range of careers, including the ones profiled in this chapter, can help you with every step of the process. In particular, they can help introduce you to options you have never considered before. The universe of career options for former lawyers is so broad that it makes the question "what can you do with a law degree" as irrelevant as the question "what can you do with the ability to read and write." As the wide range of examples in this chapter shows, you can do anything with a law degree. As Liz often tells college students who are wondering whether they should go to law school, you can also do anything without a law degree, aside from practicing law.

Starting Your Own Company

Starting your own business can be just a daydream for people who lack the skills and expertise to make that new business a reality. Because of our law school training and sometimes because of our legal experience, lawyers have the skills and expertise to create successful startups in any sector. Lawyers are always involved with startups in a counseling role, of course. Every startup needs some legal advice at nearly every stage of development, from choosing a legal form for the business to trademarking the business name to creating the kinds of contracts startups need to retain talent, formalize relationships, and protect their intellectual property. But many of the most interesting startups are run by former lawyers and have nothing to do with law.

Some of these startups become massively successful businesses. One example is the Boston Beer Company, which owns the Sam Adams beer and Angry Orchard cider brands among many others. Jim Koch, who has a JD and an MBA, started that business shortly after leaving graduate school.

Third Space Brewing may grow to match that kind of scale someday. For now, it is a smaller brewery based in Milwaukee. Third Space Brewing opened its first brewery in 2016, and started distributing beer across Wisconsin in 2021. Its co-founder, Andy Gehl, is a former lawyer. Andy is also the director of sales and marketing. The other co-founder, Kevin Wright, won the JS Ford Award, given to the world's top performer in the Institute of Brewing and Distilling's annual Brewing Exam. Kevin had years of experience brewing award-winning beer before starting Third Space Brewing with Andy. As the brewery's website explains, Andy's "legal, business and relationship building experience complement Kevin's technical brewing and operational expertise." Kevin and Andy met years ago at a YMCA summer camp in Wisconsin, the kind of "third place" that gave the brewery its name. What are your friends from summer camp doing now? Would they like to start a business with you?

Creative Partnerships

A different kind of creative partnership led to the creation of Sip & Sonder in southern California. Sip & Sonder encompasses a coffee house, coffee roastery, multi-purpose event space and creative workspace.[134] Its co-founders, Amanda-Jane Thomas and Shanita Nicholas, are both former lawyers who met while practicing at the same big Wall Street law firm. As they explained to Ellen DeGeneres when they appeared on the Ellen show in early 2021, their idea for a business grew both from their shared unhappiness practicing law and their mutual passion for coffee, comfortable and creative spaces, and promoting community. Their slogan is "For the Community, For the Culture," and they encourage people to "be you with us, wherever you are."

Their purpose in creating their business was to support the startup community by providing a space where people could not only drink coffee but also form networks and have space for creative expression. They define "sonder" as "the realization that each random passerby is living a life as vivid and complex as your own." They see Sip & Sonder as a way to bring together coffee, community, and culture in the same creative space.

Importantly, Amanda-Jane and Shanita were not miserable when they left their firm. Amanda-Jane explains that she liked practicing law, but the long hours and the nature of the work made her wonder whether that was enough.[135] She knew that there was something else, but she wasn't sure what it was. Those same long hours led to a close friendship with Shanita, and over time, they talked with each other about what their passions outside of law would look like. For Shanita, those passions included but went beyond coffee.

The strength of their shared visions gave them the impetus to develop a business plan together. In addition to working out the operational aspects of opening a business, including the financing and construction, they also worked on the fundamental question of what their brand stood for. As consumers, they thought about why they loved certain brands and not others, an issue that Amanda-Jane has described as "that broader, ephemeral, intangible, existential stuff that's also super-important and ever-evolving."[136]

Providing their own funding for the space was a critical decision. It meant that the process of opening the business took longer than it might have otherwise because they had to continue working while they created the plans. But it also meant that they had more options and control of the business because they were not beholden to outside investors. Amanda-Jane and Shanita opened the first specialty coffee house in Inglewood, California as Sip & Sonder's flagship location in 2017. In November 2021, Sip & Sonder opened its second location at the Music Center in downtown Los Angeles.

Their experience as attorneys helped in ways you might expect as well as in ways you might not expect. They could serve as Sip & Sonder's attorneys themselves, handling the immense amount of paperwork involved in starting a business, from leasing a space to handling construction contracts. Although they did not have prior experience with specific aspects of the construction like electrical wiring and plumbing, their experience negotiating on behalf of clients in other contexts helped them handle their own negotiations with contractors. Their legal experience also made them patient. Shanita noted that having called the IRS "a thousand times" over the course of her legal career prepared her well for waiting for responses from other government entities.

Both Third Space Brewing and Sip & Sonder are deeply engaged in giving back to their communities. The community-building aspect of Sip & Sonder is a prominent part of its social presence. On its website, Shanita notes that coffee shops have always played a role in fostering social relationships, which are especially important to communities of color: "[T]hese aspects of connecting, storytelling, and getting business done are hugely important to building community and culture and are uniquely found in coffee shops, which are not typically found in black communities."[137]

Senior Business Leadership

The same skills that make lawyers successful heads of startups can also serve them well at the top levels of more well established businesses. Greg Doody, President and Chief Executive Officer of Vineyard Brands, provides an example of the kind of lawyer-turned-leader path that many other unhappy lawyers may want to follow. Vineyard Brands is a successful wine importation company, and Greg has added a sommelier certification to his CPA and JD qualifications.

After graduating from law school, Greg worked as a corporate lawyer for nearly 20 years, eventually leading several high-visibility corporate restructurings. After one particular restructuring, he decided that it was time to do something else. "I tried retirement for a bit, but I was really terrible at it," he says. In an effort to keep his mind engaged in something, he enrolled in the Culinary Arts program at the French Culinary Institute (now the International Culinary Center) in New York. Although he loved the program, he did not love the career path that the training usually led to: starting a career as a chef. He learned, however, that the institute also offered an Intensive Sommelier Training program. Because he had always been passionate about wine, being steeped in the world of wine for the duration of the program sounded like an incredible opportunity. He enrolled in the next session.

As he worked his way through the program, Greg kept hearing the same advice from the Master Sommeliers who taught his classes: maybe he should go into the wine importation business. Although he was not especially eager to start a new career, he decided to learn more about the business from someone he had met at Vineyard Brands through his network. When Greg met with him to ask why so many people thought he would succeed in the business, his contact at Vineyard Brands did more than give him an answer. He offered Greg his job.

As a corporate lawyer, Greg had worked with several CEOs. He had had a chance to observe what makes a CEO successful, and he had observed CEOs who were less successful. He tried to learn from the former and avoid the mistakes of the latter.[138] Like a good lawyer, he found that successful CEOs are good at communicating about a shared goal for their team. They also take care to listen to their customers and suppliers, just as effective lawyers listen to their clients, witnesses, and everyone else who plays a role in their cases. In addition, like the leaders of good legal teams, they surround themselves with strong and effective team players.

Creative Startups

A lot of people dream of following their hearts and becoming an artist, a baker, or a filmmaker. Lawyers are better able to turn those dreams into realities than most other people because they have the practical skills needed to set up those businesses and make them successful.

For creative people who also have relatively driven, type-A personalities, law school can seem like the least awful option for graduate school. It doesn't involve blood or numbers, and it offers at least the superficial promise of making the world a better place through promoting justice. It is hard for people who have been through law school to take that perspective seriously, but it is common among new and prospective law students. So it should not be surprising that many former lawyers go out on their own to start creative businesses after practicing law.

Julie Schechter, Small Packages

Julie Schechter is the founder of Small Packages, which offers curated and unusual gift boxes for all occasions and all types of recipients.[139] Julie worked for AmeriCorps after getting her degree in Dance and Global Cultures from the University of California at

Irvine. She went to law school, she says, because she considers herself "pretty verbal" and because she expected that she "could leverage a law degree to make a difference in the world."[140] After leaving Harvard Law School, she discovered fairly quickly that the practice of law was not for her.

Julie launched Small Packages because she wanted to create something special and expressive. When friends celebrated milestones, she wanted to give them something that was tangible and that felt more personal than the care packages and gift boxes she could find online. Being able to send a physical gift was especially important in a world where so much of our communication is online. "It had to be something I could be proud to send, and not really expensive," she says. "So I figured I'd try creating it!"

In order to launch her business, Julie developed a funding strategy after figuring out how much she would need to get Small Packages up and running. Because she did not have enough money herself, she decided to crowdfund the first round of investment, and came up with a compelling video to convince friends and family to invest. She recommends crowdfunding over getting other types of investment, like angel investors. Being able to raise money from the people beyond just your core network can help demonstrate to others, in later funding stages, that there truly is a market for your product.

Having attended law school helped Julie in several ways to start and run her business. First, it helped her create a network of friends that she still keeps in touch with. It also gave her the confidence that she could figure anything out. Although she usually hands her legal work over to practicing lawyers, she can understand contracts more easily than most other people.

Katrine Moite, Photographer

Katrine Moite, a professional photographer and former corporate lawyer, also attributes some of her success to her legal training.[141] When she moved from Ukraine to the United States in 2017, Katrine left behind her legal career and started learning about photography. She offered free photography shoots to friends as a way to learn the field and to become more familiar with her new home in New York City. As a photographer, she works with clients, just as she did as a lawyer. In both photography and law, there is a need to be able to solve problems quickly and to act professionally under pressure. And in both fields, nothing is more important than making the client happy.[142]

In fact, photography may offer a better way to promote social justice than the practice of law, at least corporate law. One of Katrine's most noteworthy projects is a documentary series focused on underrepresented groups, including the residents of an Oglala Lakota Indian reservation in South Dakota. Her efforts to document life on the reservation are intended to bring attention to the problems of poverty and neglect that Native American communities face. In this way, Katrine is an advocate although she is no longer practicing law.

Loly Orozco, Postage and Paper Designer

Former lawyer Loly Orozco's design business, Little Postage House, focuses on creating the most beautiful custom stamps and invitations for clients' most important life events.[143] Until 2016, Loly was perfectly content practicing law. She describes herself as the girl who grew up watching Law & Order and dreaming of arguing her case in open court. After law school, Loly clerked for a District Court and then worked as a restructuring attorney for a major law firm. One day in 2016, however, Loly saw a bride mailing invitations with beautiful calligraphy and fine details. She realized that none of the postage stamps available were suitable for the invitations, and came up with the idea for Little Postage House.

She did not start the business right away, however. It took four years of working full time at her law firm and developing her business on the side until she could step away from her law practice entirely. Because she was already one of relatively few women in her practice area, and often the only woman at events or in court, she did not want to risk being seen as less committed to her work.

For that reason, she kept her business a secret, working on creating stamps and assembling invitations late at night and when she was free on the weekends.

And then she had to choose. Staying on the legal career path offered more certainty. "I knew where my future was heading and where I would be in five, ten, and twenty years," she said.[145] On the other hand, she had no idea where being an entrepreneur would lead. But she loves what she is doing now so much that she doesn't mind the uncertainty of following an unconventional path.

Most of her work now focuses on the creation of beautiful wedding invitations, holiday cards, and stationery. For special mailings such as invitations, she likes to tell a story about the event using vintage postage stamps and unique design elements. Sometimes that story is about the couple getting married, and sometimes the story is about the event itself, including what the guests can expect. Loly focuses on the small details in her design work to ensure that these invitations make a lasting impression on every guest from the outset.

Loly's advice to other lawyers is to be open to all possibilities. She did not plan to be an entrepreneur, but now spends every day doing something she loves and delighting her clients and their guests. While she never thought she would open a business herself, the success of Little Postage House, and Loly's own happiness, are a testament to the wisdom of keeping an open mind.

Sarah Truesdell, Baker

Sugar By Sarah is the virtual baking school run by Sarah Truesdell, a former housing attorney in Los Angeles. Sarah went to law school with the goal of becoming a public interest attorney.[146] Although she considered a number of different options, including immigration, she worked in housing rights, defending people against evictions and doing fair housing litigation. She loved being a lawyer. She enjoyed writing, working with clients, and being in court. At the same time, her family was growing. Shortly after she graduated from law school in 2008, she got married and had her first son fairly soon after that, at age 29. Then her second child arrived. In the nonprofit world, she found, there were not a lot of other lawyers who started having kids as soon as she did. She was the only female attorney around her who had children, and her supervising attorneys were less than supportive when she left at 5:30 every day. There weren't many mentors available to help her balance work and home. It was not until after she left that she was invited into a network of women lawyers who had children. Sarah wasn't comfortable with the balance in her own family, as her husband worked full time and was handling most of the elementary school logistics. It was demoralizing. Because she wasn't contributing as much as her husband was to the family income, she decided that the best thing for her and her family was to leave.

By 2016, Sarah had had enough of practicing law, and quit. She threw herself into volunteering for her children's school. Because she had always enjoyed baking, she started baking for her friends. A friend started spreading the word that Sarah was an excellent baker, and people were soon asking her to make cakes and pies for special occasions. It was energizing to get back to having the kind of creative outlet she had given up in college. Eventually, she realized that she needed to get a home baking license in order to keep doing what she loves.

Interestingly, Sarah never intended to be an entrepreneur or to work for herself. In 2018, Sarah opened Sugar by Sarah, and reporting what was initially a small income stream on her taxes. When the Covid-19 pandemic hit, Sarah decided to offer online baking classes through Facebook Live. The first time she did this, she propped up her laptop and recorded herself making sourdough bread. Some people reached out to her, requesting more lessons and specialized programs for their kids. She started to post live classes online with limited spaces for participants, and these started to sell out quickly. She realized that she needed a website[147] and to start tracking her expenses and income. By 2021, these virtual classes had become popular enough and profitable enough to constitute a full-time job.

Some aspects of teaching online baking classes are harder for her than others. She doesn't particularly like to look at herself or listen to herself, despite the wonderful feedback she gets from clients on her videos. But as a former trial attorney, she is very comfortable speaking in front of people and teaching them about the things she knows. And that helps her feel confident helping customers of all ages learn how to bake and sharing some of the joy she has found in her new career.

Anthony Desiato, Filmmaker

Or you could go in a totally different direction, like Anthony Desiato. He does not actually have a simple career description: on his LinkedIn profile, he describes himself as a "Documentarian, Podcaster, Writer, Teacher and Law School Admissions Officer."[148] At a minimum, Anthony is a former lawyer who now makes documentary films.[149]

Anthony went to the Elisabeth Haub School of Law at Pace University with a general interest in intellectual property, but no specific career plans. He had always liked writing—in fact, he had majored in journalism—and wondered whether a job in entertainment law might help him get involved in more creative work. He also acknowledges that there was "certainly some parental encouragement to go to law school."[150]

After his first year in law school, he wanted a more creative outlet for the summer. He started spending more time in a comic book store in New York called Alternate Realities.[151] His first film, My Comic Shop DocumentARy, was shown at film festivals around the country. It attracted media attention, including that of the New York Times. Bolstered by that success and enjoying his time behind the camera, Anthony went on to make an award-winning short film called By Spoon! His next film was the feature-length Wacky Man: The Rise of a Puppeteer. His most recent film, My Comic Shop Country, was funded through Kickstarter. He was able to get a distributor, and the film became available on Amazon and AppleTV.[152]

But he also used his law school experience to make more videos. After graduating, he started making videos for the administration on a freelance basis. When a position in Admissions opened up, the law school hired him. After working his way up to becoming the Director of JD Admissions, he took on a new role as the Manager of Assessment and Advising.

Anthony also hosts a podcast called My Comic Shop History. His podcasts started in 2015, when a beloved local comic shop decided to close. He wanted to chronicle the end of that particular store's era and bring in people to talk about the highlights of its history. As the podcast evolved, he began to focus more on other aspects of comics, including collections and conventions.

Having gone to law school has helped Anthony in at least two ways. First, he is comfortable handling his own licensing agreements, releases, and copyright and trademark issues. More substantively, the problem-solving skills he developed in law school apply to his work developing documentaries. When issues come up during the storyboarding, production, or any other aspect of filmmaking, Anthony's legal training helps him work through each issue systematically to find a solution.[153]

All of these examples are meant to give you just a small sampling of the options that are available to you outside the law. But each one of them is a pioneer, going in the direction that made the most sense to each former lawyer given their talents, constraints, and the many other considerations in their lives that have shaped their careers so far. Instead of looking for a pattern or prescribed path, we encourage you to chart your own path, step by step, based on your own unique talents and needs.

CHAPTER 12

On the Side: Transition Strategies for the Risk Averse

"The original business plan was to break even at 50,000 cases, but we kept growing."[154]

—Jess Jackson, lawyer turned founder of Kendall-Jackson Wines

Fighting Fire With Fear

IN 2014, A FIREFIGHTER CAPTAIN, Shayn Proler sued the City of Houston for reassigning him to administrative duties after two incidents in which he was unable to go inside a burning building with his crew. In the second incident, Proler became completely paralyzed and others on the scene reported that he "did not appear to be aware of his surroundings and that he was either frightened or in the throes of an acute medical emergency."[155]

In court, Proler argued that in reassigning him, the City had discriminated against him for a disability and had violated the Americans with Disabilities Act (ADA). The Court disagreed, noting that the ADA does not protect persons who lack the skills to perform a particular job. And further, the court noted, being afraid to run into a burning building is not a disability. It is in fact "the normal human response."[156]

You may well empathize with Captain Proler for his fear of running inside a burning building. You may even empathize with Captain Proler for wanting so badly to lead his crew, that he sought legal intervention despite clear evidence that he was a danger to himself and his crew unless reassigned. But the Court was right to protect Captain Proler and the members of his "fire suppression" team by ruling that the fire department had the right to make job assignments that were in everyone's best interests. Because let's face it, even though it doesn't make for good fire-fighting skills, it is normal for fear to hold you back from wanting to run into a burning building.

But what if fear is holding you back from running *out of one as well?* It's time for some bad news. And then some good news.

Bad News: Risk Management Is Going to Want to Hold You Back

So you've outgrown the practice of law? Or maybe you just don't love what you do anymore. Or maybe you never really loved it, but you had your reasons for going to law school that mostly revolved around parental expectations and a decent LSAT score and now ... you're a lawyer.

OK. Here's the bad news first. You know that attribute that makes you a lawyer? Your risk management skill? Your chess player mentality of looking several steps ahead to assess potential landmines to protect against? Congratulations, it's also going to be the thing that's going to hold you back from leaving the career you've come to hate.

Goli Kalkhoran, host of "Lessons From a Quitter," shares on her podcast stories of transitioning lawyers, who have time and time again worked to overcome this inherent bias against change and risk. Her podcast is one of many useful tools to add to your daily routine that can help you change your mindset with little to no time commitment (We recommend you add "Lessons From a Quitter" to your commute routine or listen over meals without adding a single additional time burden to your day). In a three-year recap episode from 2021, Kalkhoran delivers several lessons learned from interviewing three years' worth of transitioning lawyers, including that "your brain is a liar." This is a message particularly poignant for the would-be transitioning lawyer who can't seem to wrap their brain around the idea that change won't necessarily end in disaster. That leaving the law is not, in fact, the equivalent of running *into* a burning building but very well may be the opposite. Because after all, as Kalkhoran points out, what if your brain stopped delivering the hopeless message that the worst could happen if you leave the law? What if your brain got on board and reminded you that the best could happen, too?

Take for example Jess Salomon, New York-based Canadian comedian and former lawyer, who has appeared on *The Tonight Show* with Jimmy Fallon. Or Jennifer Berson, President & Founder of Jeneration PR, a Public Relations and Social Media Marketing firm specializing in promoting beauty, baby and lifestyle brands. Since leaving the law in 2005, Berson has been featured in the *New York Times, Forbes, Inc., Business Insider, Yahoo!, Entrepreneur Magazine, CBS.com, PR Week, Huffington Post, Fox 11 News, TV Guide Network's "Hollywood 411," PR Web,* and was profiled on Apple.com. Jen was also selected by Babble.com recently as one of their 10 "Mompreneurs Who Made it Big!"[157]

Take also Jason Boehmig, CEO and co-founder of the successful start-up, Ironclad, a contract lifecycle management platform that makes contract negotiation, compliance, and collaboration easier for in-house legal teams. In 2020, five years after Boehmig left the law, Ironclad was named by Forbes one of the 25 fastest-growing venture-backed startups most likely to reach a $1 billion valuation. That's right. One *billion.*

Then there's Regina Merson who left her law firm career in 2016 to start Reina Rebelde (in Spanish "rebel Queen"), a profitable makeup company geared toward Latina women, whose products are sold directly through the Reina Rebelde website and via retailers like Walmart, and which has been featured by *Forbes, O Magazine, InStyle,* and *Popsugar,* just to name a few.

And what about all those lawyers turned entrepreneurs highlighted in Chapter 11?

So. Yes, your natural, or perhaps well-honed, that's-what-makes-you-a-lawyer inclination toward risk management and risk aversion will tell you that leaving the law can be dicey. Your brain will remind you of all the things that can go wrong. But is your brain also leaving room to tell you about all the things that can go *right*? If not, let us help.

Handling the Financials

For many lawyers, the biggest obstacle to changing careers is the temporary, and sometimes permanent, drop in income that usually goes along with a professional transition. The two best ways to brace yourself for the financial impact of a career transition are to reduce your expenses gradually over time and to develop other sources of income.

You've heard of the "golden handcuffs," right? That's the term for the difficulty people have stepping away from high paying jobs once they have taken on the kinds of living expenses that those jobs make possible. Maybe they have a mortgage or private school tuition to pay. Maybe they have become accustomed to high-end restaurants every weekend or a personal shopper at their favorite clothing store. The stress and hours that go along with Big Law jobs mean that it is easy to justify those expenses, and Big Law salaries make them easy to pay for. And they don't have time to comparison shop. For many people, there is also a certain amount of misery spending that goes along with disliking your job. Having had a lousy day at work often justifies an online purchase that they don't truly need. If they can't be happy at work, at least they can have a gorgeous wardrobe or a luxurious vacation when their case wraps up.

Obviously, those expenses are unsustainable when the fancy lawyer income goes away. And that can be hard to reconcile. Professional uncertainty can be hard enough to deal with by itself without also introducing material deprivation. We have worked with many lawyers who have told us that they would change careers if only they didn't have private school tuition to pay or other fixed expenses that they could not get out of. Setting aside student loans and mortgages, which are harder to get out of than other expenses, everything else is negotiable.

Reducing expenses is one of the most liberating things you can do if you are even thinking about an alternative career. Even school tuition, which seems intractable, can be negotiated if your financial situation changes such that you become more eligible for financial aid.

The complement to reducing expenses, of course, is increasing income. The easiest way to do this is by taking on gig work that you do just for the money. Kevin Han, founder of the Financial Panther blog, chronicled the strategies he used to pay off his student loans. His blog reflects a running tally of the money he has made from side hustles.[158] He makes every little bit, including signup bonuses from banks and credit cards, count toward paying down his debt. He also chronicles and reviews his experiences with a wide range of part-time gigs, including driving for delivery and rideshare companies.

Another way to start bringing in income is to develop your own business. This is something you can do before you leave your law job. If you are considering becoming an entrepreneur, it is something you <u>should</u> do before you leave a secure and steady income. Experimenting with a business on the side is an excellent way to figure out whether you will be able to replace part or all of your income with a new business. No amount of theoretical calculation can substitute for the actual experience of doing the work you think you will love, finding customers, paying your overhead expenses, and dealing with the administration necessary to make any business work.

Good News: You Already Have What You Need to Transition From the Law.

First things first. You may not actually be as risk averse as you think. As Olga Mack, CEO of Parley Pro, a contract management company, has pointed out, the idea that all lawyers are risk averse, may be more cliche than universal truth.[159] In fact, we have seen time and time again that the law attracts very creative people and then gives them little or no outlet for that creativity. In large firms especially, creative solutions are neither incentivized nor rewarded. The status quo is not easily challenged and so lawyers are often thwarted in seeking creating endeavors and solutions.

Does this mean, then, that lawyers are less risk averse and more risk forbidden? Possibly. And maybe it's a distinction without substance, so we want to be careful not to belabor the point, while still reminding you that just because people are always telling you lawyers are risk averse doesn't mean it's true. And it doesn't mean it's true for you.

Similarly, just because people are always telling you it's too risky to give up your law career for another dream doesn't mean it's true. And it doesn't mean it's true for you. What is true is that there is risk involved in transitioning from the law, and there are ways to manage that risk to acceptable levels. Ever since we started counseling transitioning lawyers, we have been delivering a consistent message: if you want to explore an alternative career in a completely risk-averse manner, you can. Just try it out on the side.

Cultivate a hobby that will take you outside your usual networking circle. Volunteer for a nonprofit to get a behind-the-scenes look at the company's operations and needs. Join the Board of a growing start-up and see if the entrepreneurial life is for you without quitting your day job.

It's a seemingly foolproof method of exploring life beyond law for the risk averse, and yet, again and again we hear from lawyers as they lament that the barrier holding them back from pursuing *anything* on the side is *time*.

While this issue of *time* is a real concern, we have a real solution. You may not realize it yet, but one of the most useful tools you have from working in private practice is your ability to manage your time. After all, you do it every day, competitively and successfully. That's right, the thing that you just might consider the bane of your existence, is going to come in handy if you want to transition successfully from the law: *the billable hour model*.

Hear us out. The simple fact is that lawyers are pros at compartmentalizing their time in small blocks to achieve efficiency and productivity, and that skill can guide you through an exploratory transition phase as well if you let it. Set aside and carefully schedule three to five hours per week at first (increasing as you go along) to shift gears from your practice to career transition tasks. Spend these blocks of time on specific tasks: research, networking phone calls, or meetings. Volunteer. Get your foot in the door of some businesses and companies you want to learn more about. Importantly, you need to write these additional hours into your schedule. Treat them as new matters and cultivate them as such.

Eventually you might even find ways to monetize your side activities. Don't believe us? Just ask Kevin Han, the creator of Financial Panther, a blog mentioned earlier in this chapter about personal finance, travel hacking, and side hustling that was originally created alongside his legal career. By carving out time on the side, Kevin gradually learned how to leverage the sharing economy to integrate various side gigs into his monthly revenue sources including renting out extra rooms via airbnb, signing up for rideshare, survey, and delivery apps, and dog walking/dog sitting. He claims that his participation in various side gigs has led to financial freedom, and ultimately the evolution of Financial Panther into a full-time position. In fact, Kevin documents what he earns—to the penny—each month in these various endeavors. And now, since 2019, his side hustle has become *the hustle*.[160]

Kevin told us about his leap from the law:

"I quit my job in 2019 to pursue full-time blogging and gig economy work. At the time I made the leap into self-employment, I had been practicing law for five years, first at a large law firm, then in state government, and then, in my last job, at a non-profit. I think I did what a lot of lawyers do, where I was looking for some perfect job within the legal field, when in reality, I probably wasn't going to find what I was looking for as a lawyer."

Kevin started side hustling, mainly by using gig economy apps, as an outlet from the law. He was fitting in jobs alongside his life, delivering food while biking and dog sitting while he was taking care of his dog. Kevin explained: "I found that a lot of these on-demand gig economy apps worked really well for me. I could turn them on whenever I wanted, work for as long or as little as I wanted, and basically make extra money on my own time. Importantly, I found that a lot of these apps could fit into the things I was already doing."

Eventually, Kevin started Financial Panther. He wrote it anonymously while practicing law from 2016-2019. Over time, the blog continued to grow and in 2019, Kevin "decided to take a leap and shift my focus entirely to my blog."

Kevin's decision to look outside the law for side gigs might seem a bit unorthodox until you consider that it's consistent with a nationwide trend. *ABA Journal's* Jenny Davis reported in 2018 that as many as 1 in 5 American workers are actually taking on side jobs, in part to make additional income.[161] But there can be additional benefits as well. And sometimes, as we see in the case of Kevin's Financial Panther, the side gigs can become independent sources of revenue.

Wayback Burger Chief Development Officer, Bill Chemero, believes that exploring side opportunities can help open your eyes to careers you might not have thought to pursue otherwise and has some good advice for doing so.[162] Chemero points out that new businesses can be cultivated online from scratch with just a hobby or an idea. And he also points out that there are career coaches, and other professionals that can help you with the necessary steps to start your business. Nevertheless, he suggests you try out the business before jumping in. "For instance," he says, "if you want to start a coffeehouse, you might get a part-time job at a coffeehouse first to get a sense of whether this is really living the dream or you just really like the smell of coffee."[163]

In many cases, exploratory side hustles are unrelated to "day jobs." And for lawyers, these side hustles generally *must* be unrelated to their law firm gigs for ethics and conflict of interest reasons.[164] In an ABA Journal article "These lawyers balance full-time practices with a side hustle that pays," Dennis A. Rendleman, lead senior ethics counsel at the ABA's Center for Professional Responsibility in Chicago, pointed out that:

"It's ... important to be mindful of overlaps between law practice and business activity ... Generally, the more lawyers separate their law practices from their side jobs, the less likely they are to run into ethics issues. It all comes down to intent ... If the intent of the side venture is unconnected to promoting the lawyer's practice or soliciting clients, the chances of an ethics violation lessen."[165]

While Kevin Han eventually turned his side hustles into a lucrative full-time job, leaving the law for good in 2019, other lawyers report a desirable balance between their active practice and side gig for quite some time. Take for example, Rho Thomas, who is still practicing (albeit at a reduced schedule) alongside financial coaching for lawyers. Thomas says: "My mission is to empower women lawyers with the knowledge and tools to regain control of their time, build wealth, and live the lives of freedom and choice they deserve."

Mary Cobb is currently a practicing attorney at O'Melveny & Myers and also a self-taught artist whose work has been exhibited in Rome, the Berkshires, and D.C. She keeps balance in her legal career by feeding her creative spirit through painting, a vocation she took up during a sabbatical from the law in 2013. Mary lived in Rome from 2013-2016, immersed in her craft, returning to the U.S. in 2016 and returning to the law as well. She continues to balance her art with her practice of law, a fact made more interesting since her art has been described as "lawless."[169]

Christina Previte is an attorney, CEO and co-founder of New Jersey Divorce Solutions, working to develop alternative ways to help make divorce less costly and less traumatic. Christina is also the Host of the *Wake Up Call Podcast*. She believes her mission "is to help other people adjust their mindset and perceptions that only serve as blind spots to their living their best life."[170]

As we see from examples such as those above, side ventures can be enough to bring your law practice into focus. They can create balance and for some, maintaining both is desirable. Be prepared, however, for things to occasionally get "out of balance" when you're pursuing a side venture.

Consider the story of Nina Lacher. Lacher started the Law of Fashion Blog in 2014 while practicing law as a civil litigator, with the intention of differentiating herself from other bloggers and monetizing the site quickly. She did both, including by incorporating fashion "laws" into her posts and growing her readership and social media followings in order to attract big name sponsors. As of February 2022, she had over 300,000 Instagram followers and had partnered with the likes of DSW, Toyota, Payless ShoeSource, Marriott, and Hertz.[171]

In 2018, when interviewed for an article for ABA Journal, Lacher was still blogging alongside her law practice (and alongside mothering a new baby as well). At that time, she claimed she'd never leave the practice of law. "I put a lot of time and effort into being an attorney, and I would never leave that, and I have a client base that I can't walk away from ... [P]eople will always need lawyers, and I could never 100 percent give that up."[172] But a year later, Lacher changed her mind and decided that the blog was successful enough to take the leap to full-time blogging, leaving the law behind.

On the flip side, consider also, Vanessa Perlman, who has explored a travel biz alongside her law gig. For five years, she ran Mockingbird Travel,[173] a travel company with a philanthropic bent, while still working as a freelance lawyer. Following the start of the pandemic, she realized a need to pivot away from the travel industry, and her professional balance shifted back to law: away from a freelance model in either realm.[174] As Vanessa points out, while freelance work in her legal world allowed flexibility to pursue her side gig, it didn't give her the security or stability she needed to pursue it wholeheartedly. "Honestly, it was hard," Perlman admits.[175]

Which it is. But it's not so hard that it's not worth trying. Gretchen Rubin, a lawyer turned New York Times bestselling writer of *The Happiness Project*, first realized she wanted to be a writer while clerking for Justice Sandra Day O'Connor, and says that the first step to a happier life generally involves some action.[176]

In fact, Amy recalls the first step she took to becoming a professional writer was inspired by a meme that flashed across her screen one day scrolling through social media. It read simply: "You know all those things you've wanted to do? You should go do them." She started her "Author" blog the very same day and within a year had a modest but loyal following and her first publishing contract: a contract from ABA Publishing for *Lawyer Interrupted*.

Put simply, the time is there for modest side activity even now, and because you, our dear lawyer friends, already know how to effectively and efficiently manage your time, we have no doubt you can soon trade your billable hours for hours that work for you instead.

Doing It on the Side is Actually Good for You

Still not convinced you have the time in your schedule to set aside for exploring alternatives to the practice of law? What if we told you that exploring alternatives to your daily practice was actually good for you? That it would help your brain grow and develop and aid in your ultimate transition? (Or it might help you to refocus your career in the law if you ultimately decide to stay.)

Here's the scoop. The ability of the human brain to develop new neurons or new paths in response to stimulation and learning is referred to as neuroplasticity.[177] Neuroplasticity is how the brain overcomes trauma and creates resilience needed to, among other things, grow old gracefully.[178] Notably, recent scientific research centering around neuroplasticity has challenged the old way of thinking that cognitive aging is fixed, and there's nothing to be done to offset the brain's cognitive deficits during the aging process. Instead, in a 2016 scientific journal article, the authors concluded that: "On balance, the available evidence favors the hypothesis that maintaining an intellectually engaged and physically active lifestyle promotes successful cognitive aging."[179]

Pursuing new ventures outside the law is not risky for your mental health. Instead, it can improve it dramatically. And what happens if you have to route and reroute and pivot a few times before you find your way to a successful law transition? All the better!

Consider this. A study of London cab drivers concluded that their brains literally grow by having to reroute on a daily basis. "A cab driver's hippocampus—the part of the brain that holds spatial representation capacity—is measurably larger than that of a bus driver. By driving the same route every day, the bus drivers don't need to exercise this part of the brain as much. The cabbies, on the other hand, rely on it constantly for navigation."[180,181]

Once you accept that you do indeed have time to devote to a side venture, and once you accept that the risk can be minimized to an acceptable level, to a level that is not harmful, and in fact, might actually be good for you, you can start looking for the right side gig.

When the Transition From Side Gig Is Complete

You may wonder when you'll know. When will the new directions and rerouting lead to a full transition from the law? While we think it looks differently for every transitioning lawyer, we do think there's some universal wisdom to extrapolate from the story of Peter J. Kim, Founding Director of the Museum of Food and Drink in Brooklyn, New York.

Peter came to the law after a term in the Peace Corps, where he briefly entertained, and then rejected a future in international development, after bearing witness to a high level of corruption (outside of the Peace Corps). After seeing, however, what an absence of a cohesive legal system created in the various places he traveled, he was inspired to go to law school, use what he learned, and maybe even "do some good in the world," Peter says.

He landed first in Big Law in New York City, in a niche field of international disputes. Peter describes his position as intellectually challenging but still he looked at the partners' lives around him, and decided early on that law firm life was not his end destination.

He didn't form an immediate exit strategy. Instead, he made it a goal to "nurture my personal passions." For many years, he'd been a foodie and a music enthusiast, having explored the cultural narrative behind food as a world traveler, Peace Corps member, and hobbyist chef (in undergrad school, Peter discovered *On Food and Cooking* by McGee which he describes as enormously impactful). While practicing law, he attended culinary school on weekends, ran a supper club out of his apartment and immersed himself in the food and music world in New York City; so much so, in fact, that when he received an invitation to a fundraising event for a new concept called the Museum of Food and Drink, he immediately accepted.

After the lunch, Peter was convinced the Museum was well on its way to coming together. Still, he was not quite able to let go of the idea of being part of it. Peter remembers emailing founder Dave Arnold, "on a lark," letting Arnold know that if he needed any legal help, Peter would see what he could do about bringing the museum project on as a *pro bono* case at his Big Law law firm. Arnold took him up on his offer immediately, and Peter realized the museum was still very much just an idea. He pitched it to his firm, got approval to take the project on as a *pro bono* gig, formed a team, and a year later went the extra step of suggesting Arnold find a full-time director for the museum.

Peter says he didn't see himself in that role at first, but eventually, when he became concerned that this project he'd become so vested in might not come to fruition, he took a look in the mirror, and decided to take on the Founding Director position himself. The partners thought he was crazy when he resigned, and Peter himself admits to many moments when he was afraid they were right.

To deal with the financial hurdle, he relied on the little savings he'd amassed in Big Law, though Peter says he wishes he'd saved more. He reports being "wildly optimistic" about how quickly he'd be able to draw a salary from the museum position, and says he'd advised others following his story to be a bit more practical and realistic. Ultimately, he subsidized the museum directorship through side gigs not unlike Kevin Han of the Financial Panther, utilizing Airbnb to rent out loft space in his New York City apartment, and sometimes the apartment itself, a move he describes as necessary and difficult. "I had this glamorous museum director position by day and then by night, I'd have to come home and unclog toilets. It was humbling."

Still, Peter says he found value in the museum project, in the act of building something from the ground up, and when he finally made up his mind to move on from the museum position, he took a position with Pinterest, staking out a spot in the pivot of the company from being a tool to curate ideas to a content-creation platform for big ideas.

"It's still about building something," Peter says, and so, notwithstanding the move from small nonprofit to big tech, his experience with the museum is still very much relevant, as is his legal training as he works with the legal team at Pinterest on contract review and modification relating to the new pivot.

Peter says even though he knew he wouldn't likely stay at Big Law forever, he wasn't miserable, an indication that he probably left in the Goldilocks window of "just right" (although he admits he wishes he'd saved just a bit more cash for the transition to museum director since he wasn't able to draw a salary for about a year after the leap).

Notably, Peter also says that around the time he moved to Pinterest, about eight years after leaving the law, he finally decided to stop paying bar dues and keeping up with CLEs. The transition from the law felt complete at that point. "It's such a low bar to keep your status as active, I figure when you don't even want to meet that low bar, it's telling." Peter says he knows now "there's no scenario" that will have him practicing law again, and that's all right. Does he still think of himself as a lawyer? "No," Peter replies. "It's really just a fun fact at this point."

That brings us back to our original question that started this discussion. When will *you* know your transition is complete? Well, it might look different to everyone; certainly when it's no longer central to your identity, but rather a fun fact, you've gotten a head start.

CHAPTER 13

You Don't Have to Go It Alone

(A Guide to Finding and Using the Right Career Coach to Aid in Your Transition)

"I'm not looking 20 years down the road, not even five, I care about this year."[182]

—Jon Cooper, Public Defender turned 2x Stanley Cup Winning NHL Coach

Don't Get Into a Sticky Situation: Do Your Research

IN 2021, THE UNFORTUNATE PLIGHT of a young woman who substituted her usual hair spray product, Got2B Glued, for a household adhesive, Gorilla Glue, went viral on Tik Tok, as she sought to have the latter removed from her scalp through various methods. Eventually, Ms. Brown required medical attention.[183]

Because both products used by Ms. Brown undeniably have the word "glue" in the name, and notably, there is another popular hair product known affectionately as "Gorilla Snot," Ms. Brown went public with her experience to ensure that others don't get confused or try substituting Gorilla Glue for hair gel or spray. She even set up a GoFundMe account to help with wigs and medical costs. While she asked for $1,500, the fund quickly raised over $20,000.

Reports that Ms. Brown was using the funds fraudulently or that she was planning to go so far as to sue Gorilla Glue for her mistake, all turned out to be unfounded. Instead, Ms. Brown donated funds raised in the GoFundMe campaign to Restore, a nonprofit organization providing reconstructive surgery to battered and abused children around the world. Restore's founder, Dr. Michael Obeng, was the one who performed restorative procedures on Ms. Brown's scalp, *pro bono*, after the Gorilla Glue misuse.[184]

Gorilla Glue issued a public statement on its social media channels expressing regret about Ms. Brown's experience, and also noting that the mistake could have been avoided by careful label reading and research: "Our spray adhesive states in the warning label 'Do not swallow. Do not get in eyes, on skin, or on clothing....'"[185]

While we agree with commentators observing that Ms. Brown's predicament provides a larger discussion prompt regarding difficult, and sometimes unrealistic beauty standards, we also think this story provides another important lesson:

Always read the label and do your research before committing. This is especially important in the area of legal career coaching.

Put Me in, Coach

The life coaching industry is a relatively young one, having emerged on the scene only in the last 20 years or so, with legal coaching appearing much more recently.[185] Indeed when we released *Lawyer Interrupted* and *Life After Law*, there were hardly any widely recognized coaches regularly helping lawyers, and most transitioning lawyers were going it alone. In the last decade, however, the rising number of successful coaches—and in particular, the rising number of successful lawyers-turned-coaches—has had a big, and we believe, favorable, impact on the legal industry.

Coaching, in general, is an industry that appears to have threaded itself into the American market with some vigor. For example, the market value of the coaching industry is predicted to reach USD 1.34 billion by the year 2022.[186] Forbes has touted the universal value of coaching. "Coaching is incredibly helpful for everyone's development path, not just those in the C-suite."[187]

It's not just individuals—and not just lawyers!—who are looking for help from the coaching industry. In fact, 25% to 40% of all Fortune 500 companies include executive coaching as a part of their standard leadership training for their top executives and best performers.[188]

To be clear, we think the use of a career coach can be invaluable to the transition process; but we caution you to do your homework and carefully research potential coaches. The coaching industry is unregulated and there are approximately 500 coaching certification programs currently available.[189] Two biggies are the International Coaching Federation (ICF) and The Center for Credentialing and Education (CCE). Both have a code of ethics.[190] Yet, opinions differ on what is truly the "gold standard" in the coaching certification world.

In this growing and ever-changing, dynamic field, we think there are important considerations in choosing your coach, including: (1) whether the coach was previously a lawyer, (2) the strategies employed by the coach, (3) the services/accessibility offered by the coach, (4) the experience of the coach and/or relevant success stories, and (5) the awareness of the coach that they are not your therapist.

We also note that coaching is not a one-size-fits-all experience. The strategies and modalities for coaching that benefit *you* may or may not work for your colleague down the hall looking to also leave the law and the barriers to entry for the field are relatively low. So, while word-of-mouth is an important reference, be sure you understand just why a particular transitioning lawyer is referring his/her coach to you before hiring that coach yourself.

Former Lawyers Can Make Excellent Coaches

There are exceptions to every rule, except possibly this one: former lawyers make the best coaches for other lawyers. Put simply, lawyers have specific skill sets to translate beyond the legal world and specific psychological challenges that are best faced in collaboration with someone who can relate to and empathize with the career path you've been on.

Annie Little, founder of JD Nation, a successful coaching program that includes small group and one-on-one work recalls working with a non-lawyer when she was first making the transition from the practice of law nearly a decade ago. She realized quickly that the trauma experienced by lawyers who have burned out in practice is one that is not necessarily experienced in other fields. This realization eventually led her to want to start her own coaching program exclusively for lawyers.

Similarly, Rho Thomas says she "... got into helping lawyers with their money because of my personal financial struggles. My husband and I had found ourselves in over $670,000 of debt, and I was sharing our journey out of debt on a blog. Around the same time, I was having conversations with other lawyers who were making good money but struggling and feeling like they couldn't afford to do anything different. I knew I could help because of all I was learning with my own finances. Helping those first few lawyers led me to starting a business to help more lawyers, and I eventually left the law to pursue coaching full time. No one should feel stuck in a position they no longer want to be in because of money."

And consider this: as a starting point, hiring a lawyer-turned-coach can be efficient at a time when you are already questioning whether you have time to even think about transitioning. There's a shorthand between two lawyers communicating about their shared past experience that will free up more time to explore the most important issue at hand: *what comes next.*

What's the Game Plan?

When looking for a coach, it's important to understand what their strategy is, and how it will suit you personally. Before you hire a coach, make sure you also understand your own goals and preferences by asking yourself the following questions:

- Are you looking for structure versus free-flowing style?

- Are you looking for homework or regular (or irregular check-ins) only?

- Are you looking for a standardized assessment to kick off your working relationship? Are you looking for accountability, measurable goals, or something more fluid?

- How concerned are you about confidentiality?

If the last point is important to you, be sure you understand how confidentiality will be handled with any coach you are considering. Is there a non-disclosure agreement? Does the coach have an assistant or other employees with access to your information? How will your privacy be protected?

At the end of the day, there's no right way. There's just *their* way. And you'll need to assess honestly whether it can work for you.

JD Nation's Annie Little describes her methodology as follows:

"Treat your transition like an experiment. With an experiment there's no failure, just data.

"You've formed a hypothesis about the type of job you want next. Now go out and test your hypothesis (in a low-stakes way) so you have some data to analyze. Talk to people who have already done what you want to do. Find out how to get hands-on experience so you can experience how it feels to actually do the work. Join trade organizations.

"Next, analyze your experience. What did you learn? How did you feel? Was it what you expected? Better? Worse? Do you need to gather more data to reach a conclusion?

Based on your findings, you'll either (1) be ready to go all in on your new career or (2) realize it's not such a great fit for you and be so glad you tested out your idea before making a major change."

Candace Alnaji recommends focusing clearly on your intention for transitioning. Says Candace:

"Set your intentions and write it down. To transition successfully, a client must truly ground themselves in the reason for the transition. A client must feel a deep connection to their transition goal and take ownership over it. Without doing this, a career changer may feel compelled to continuously second guess themselves during the initial phases of their transition, and perhaps again later on the other side of it. To avoid falling victim to the "what ifs" it's important to understand your deepest "why" and to be willing to take the steps to get there, understanding that there might be speed bumps along the way."

Greg Yates, owner of Professional Career Transitions, focuses on networking and contact building as an integral part of the transition process. Yates encourages clients to spread the word. "Let everyone in your current relationship/acquaintance network know about your transition by phone, text, or email (not just a social media post) and stay in touch with them." Rho Thomas, in contrast, focuses on the financial hurdles holding many lawyers back from transitioning, helping them get their debt under control so they can feel more free to leave the law.

Sometimes the strategy is as simple (or as hard!) as a mindset shift. Annie Little notes that:

"When it comes to the fears that commonly surround leaving the law—they won't be good at anything else, they don't have any transferable skills, people will think they couldn't hack it as a lawyer, they'll disappoint their family—it's important to validate those fears while also recognizing that they often represent the worst case scenario. Our legal training turned our brains into impeccable issue spotters with an enhanced negativity bias. We can identify problems in our sleep!

"By understanding that's our lawyer brain's default state, we can learn to notice when we're focusing on the negative outcomes. The next step is to ask ourselves, 'What could go right if I leave the practice of law?' That shift in perspective can be incredibly powerful when we're feeling frozen by our fears."

Bryce Legal has an entire team dedicated to resume building and Linked In development for lawyer career transition.[191] Their strategy is primarily one of reframing and storytelling.[192]

If your prospective coach has been through a certification program, research the program itself (in addition to the coach) to explore the ecosystem, values, and ethics of that program. Don't be taken in by the certification itself, since certification programs vary in their levels of depth and difficulty. Be careful to avoid coaches who pride themselves on an "accreditation" that is given to anyone who pays the program fees without any objective evaluation at all.

In sum, whatever the strategy your prospective coach uses, make sure you know what it is. And make sure it's the right fit for *you*.

How Much or How Little?

Obviously, cost should be a consideration. You should be clear about your coach's fees/rates from the start, but more importantly, you should be clear about the value of those services as well. Will there be group sessions, one-on-one counseling, or all of the above? Will there be a free or low-cost initial session or session(s) while you explore whether this particular coach is indeed "the one"?

Annie Little offers a year-long program with regularly scheduled office hours that are often used for resume review, exploring non-traditional avenues to the practice of law, and other mentoring. While the program does not need to take a year, Little explains that she agrees to make herself available for the year so her clients can take the course on their own timelines.

Some coaches utilize the group mentoring model, and others take a birds-eye view approach to mentoring via podcasts, etc. Little notes that confidentiality is imperative in group settings, especially for lawyers who are still working "day jobs" while they explore possible transitions.

Ask yourself whether one-on-one work is important to you for confidentiality or other reasons. Ask yourself whether you want to benefit from group interactions with, and the shared experiences of, others who are similarly situated to you. Do you want one or the other or a hybrid of both? Be honest with yourself and your needs and find a coach who employs the modes of coaching/communication that will work best for you.

Maybe one-on-one isn't cost-effective because you aren't sure yet what you want. How about a community? A collective? Simple Courage offers just that. Founded by Heather Hubbard, it's not one-on-one coaching, but another model altogether. Join a Simple Courage collective and you can expect: "... unfiltered advice, practical tools, peer feedback, genuine connections, and a realness you've never experienced in another group setting before ... During this 3-month journey, you'll meet weekly with your small group Collective for 11 weeks and implement on your own for 3 weeks."

Is accountability important to you? If so, you might need an outside coach, but if you trust yourself to commit to the process without outside collaboration, then there might be another option available to you. Called "self-coaching" by Jan Newman, this method is to canvas the websites of the coaches for available resources, including podcast interviews, articles, etc. We've assembled a non-exclusive list of coaching sites/contacts to get you started in the Appendix to this book.

And if you're looking for an even more stripped-down version of coaching support, try mindfulness and/or meditation Apps such as: Headspace, Calm, Stop, Breathe & Think, or Tactical Breather.

According to Headspace's About Us: "Through science-backed meditation and mindfulness tools, Headspace helps you create life-changing habits to support your mental health and find a healthier, happier you." Not just for lawyers, or even just for transitioning professionals, Headspace boasts physical results that can help even the most stressed-out lawyers. "Headspace is proven to reduce stress by 14% in just 10 days. It can also help you relax your mind in minutes, improve focus, and get the best sleep ever."[193]

Calm is an app for "Sleep, Meditation and Relaxation," boasting that "Calm users who used the app 5x a week saw an improvement in their mental health."[194] Stop Breathe and Think and Tactical Breather are two other apps focused on wellness and mindfulness.

DO Also Get a Therapist

Annie Little says if you have to choose between hiring a therapist and hiring a coach, she'd recommend a therapist every time.

> "For most of us lawyers, our identity is deeply intertwined with our vocation. Separating ourselves from our occupation can come with a lot of intense emotions, especially grief. Even when someone is eager to leave the legal profession, they may feel a sense of loss around the idea of who they thought they would become."

For these reasons, Annie points out that the line between coaching and therapy should remain clear. Coaches should not play at being your therapist, and you, as the client should be clear that you've got the proper team of support by hiring both a coach *and* a therapist.

So how can you tell the difference between the roles of your coach and your therapist so that the lines stay clear? Therapy, unlike the coaching biz, is indeed a regulated field requiring an advanced degree and proper state licensure. And in broad strokes, your therapist often focuses on events past, while your coach looks forward. But not always. Importantly, therapy focuses on healing and self-awareness, while coaching focuses on growth and success in a time-limited slice of life.

When in doubt, sign up for therapy first, so you'll be ready for coaching next.

Measures of Success

It's helpful to discuss with your prospective coach(es) what the measurable metrics for success will be, and have them give some examples of success stories from their recent past.

Check out their website for testimonials. Look at social media channels to see what kind of engagement they have from supposed clients. If testimonials aren't available on the website, ask for names of clients to reach out. Most successful coaches will have at least a handful of clients who are willing to speak to you or communicate via email. The absence of testimonials, especially for a lawyer new to coaching, may not be a fatal flaw, but it is a consideration.

In the end, only you can truly measure your own success, but it will be helpful to have a partner in the process who is on the same page.

Be Flexible and Patient

According to Little, sometimes clients surprise even themselves. About 60% of her prospective clients come to her saying that they want to leave the law for ... the law. In other words, they often state that they want to go in-house, or get another JD-required or JD-preferred gig. In reality, many of these clients end up pivoting altogether. When they stay flexible, they often discover another profession outside of the practice of law, but that is no less fulfilling.

Conversely, some coaching clients actually decide to stay in the law and work to improve their situation from the inside, armed with the insights and reflection gained in the coaching process. Little notes that when she first started coaching:

"I wanted to work exclusively with lawyers because I knew so many brilliant people whose talents were underappreciated by the existing law firm/legal department model. While practicing law wasn't a good fit for me, I understood that many lawyers truly do want to have a lengthy legal career. The treatment they receive during the course of their careers, however, is detrimental to their physical, emotional, and mental well-being and unsustainable in the long term. I wanted to help make the practice of law more hospitable to human life!

"My long-term, lofty aspiration was to help the next generation of lawyers (mainly Millennials like me) to reform the legal profession as they ascended to leadership roles. If we couldn't effectuate meaningful top-down change (the 'old guard' at the top has zero incentive to do so), the next best thing would be to initiate change from inside the associate ranks. As my Millennial cohorts have risen to the ranks of partner and general counsel, I've had the honor of working with them as they develop into the leaders, managers, and mentors they always wished they'd had. Slowly but surely they're becoming catalysts for reform within their organizations."

If you're patient and don't lose hope if transition does not happen as quickly as you want, coaching can be a great catalyst of change from without or within.

Interviewing a Potential Coach

If you are set on hiring a coach, make sure that you understand as much as possible about them before you commit. To help, we have compiled a list of interview questions to ask the prospectives on your list:

- Can you describe your own journey from lawyer to coach?

- What was the motivation for becoming a coach?

- Why do you want to coach me?

- Has your mission as coach changed in any significant way since you first started? If so, why?

- What adversities have you faced as a coach? How do you deal with them?

- What was your most successful moment as a coach?

- What's your coaching philosophy?

- What is your coaching style?

- How often will we communicate, how will we communicate?

- How structured will it be?

- How do we achieve accountability?

- How do we measure success?

- Who is your coach/mentor?

The important thing to remember is that this is your path. It is unique. It is all your own. But you do not need to take these next steps alone. Reach out to a career coach, a trusted colleague, or an alumnus of your firm to say out loud what you've been thinking for some time now. Maybe, just maybe, it's time to learn how to leave the law.

APPENDIX A
DIRECTORY OF COACHES FOR LAWYERS

*Please note that we don't any endorse any one coach listed below. Nor do we hold this list out as an exhaustive one. We do, however, endorse doing your research, finding a coach with a style that fits your needs and goals (*See Chapter 13 for help in interviewing potential coaches*), and giving preference to a former lawyer-turned-coach. Thus we have limited our coaching directory here to former lawyers. Good luck! - Liz & Amy

Candace Alnaji
Founder, The Mom At Law, PLLC
https://themomatlaw.com

Casey Berman
Founder, Leave the Law
https://go.leavelawbehind.com

Shauna C. Bryce
Founder and Principal, Bryce Legal
https://www.brycelegal.com

Francesca Chang
Founder, Attorney on a Journey, LLC
https://www.attorney-on-a-journey.com

Sarah Cottrell
Lawyer Career Coach & Consultant |
Host of The Former Lawyer Podcast
https://formerlawyer.com

Elena Deutsch
Founder and CEO, WILL – Women Interested in Leaving (big) Law.
https://womeninterestedinleavinglaw.com

Jay Harrington
President, Harrington Communications
https://www.hcommunications.biz

Heather Hubbard
Founder and Chief Storyteller, Simple Courage
https://simplecourage.com

Goli Kalkhoran
Founder & Podcast Host, Lessons From a Quitter
https://lessonsfromaquitter.com

Annie Little
Founder, JD Nation
https://www.thejdnation.com

Jessica Medina
Founder, Jessica Medina, LLC
https://www.jessicamedinallc.com

Jan Newman
Founder, Dr. Jan Newman
https://www.jannewmancoaching.com

Megan Smiley
Founder, Megan Smiley Coaching
https://megansmiley.com

Rho Thomas
Founder, Rho Thomas, LLC
https://www.rhothomas.com

Wendi Weiner
Founder, The Writing Guru
https://writingguru.net/wendi-weiner/

Greg Yates
Founder, Greg Yates Consulting
https://www.gregyatesconsulting.com

ENDNOTES

1 "How This Lawyer-Turned-Designer Brings Black Girl Magic Into Her Business," *Faire* (June 17, 2020)

2 Debra Cassens Weiss, "BigLaw Laid Off More than 12,000 People in 2009, the Worst Year Ever," *ABA Journal* (Jan 4, 2010).

3 Dan Roe, "At More Than a Dozen Firms, 2020 Layoffs Were Followed by Partner Profit Windfalls," *Law.com* (March 4, 2021).

4 Christine Simmons, " Remote Work Has Permanently Altered Law Firm Life, for Better and for Worse," *Law.com*, April 13, 2021.

5 https://www.abalegalprofile.com/.

6 "Growing ALSP market becoming less 'alternative', says new report," *Thomson Reuters* (Feb 11, 2021).

7 "Taking the 'Alternative' out of Alternative Legal Service Providers," *The Practice, Harvard Law School* (Vol. 5, Issue 5, July/August 2019).

8 "Alternative Careers," *Berkeley Law* (https://www.law.berkeley.edu/careers).

9 University of Houston Law Center Faculty (Renee Knake Jefferson).

10 "Trends in Graduate Student Loan Debt, *NCES Blogs* (Aug 2, 2018).

11 Robert Morse, Kenneth Hines, Eric Brooks, Juan Vega-Rodriguez, and Ari Castonguay, "Methodology: 2022 Best Law Schools Rankings," *U.S. News & World Report.*

12 Ambrosio Rodriguez, "JD detours: Alternative career paths for lawyers," *ABA For Law Students* (Dec 3, 2018).

13 "Leverage & Pivot: Taking Your Legal Identity to the Next Level," *ABA Alternative Legal Careers.*

14 Student and Alumni Handouts, NALP (nalp.org).

15 Susan Smith Blakely, "Are women lawyers paying enough attention to upward mobility?" *ABA Journal* (June 29, 2021).

16 Note that the names of some of the female lawyers in this chapter have been changed, but not the details or stories.

17 Roberta D. Liebenberg and Stephanie A. Scharf, *"Walking Out the Door: The Facts, Figures and Future of Experienced Women Lawyers in Private Practice,"* (ABA & ALM Intelligence 2019).

18 "Moving Beyond Biglaw As A Single Mom Of Twins With Jessica Medina," *Former Lawyer Podcast with Host, Sarah Cottrell* (TFLP 059).

19 Susan Smith Blakely, "Are women lawyers paying enough attention to upward mobility?" *ABA Journal* (June 29, 2021).

20 *Id.*

21 *Id.*

22 Patricia Lee Refo, "Women's success in legal careers: Lack of advancement is not a 'woman' problem, it's a 'profession' problem," *ABA Journal* (July 6, 2021).

23 *Id.*

24 *Id.*

25 *Id.*

26 "Exclusive Interview with Susan Smith Blakely: Her Response to the ABA Journal Article," *Wake Up Call Podcast with Host, Christina Previte* (Episode 82: July 21, 2021).

27 Roberta D. Liebenberg and Stephanie A. Scharf, *"Walking Out the Door: The Facts, Figures and Future of Experienced Women Lawyers in Private Practice,"* (ABA & ALM Intelligence 2019).

28 *Id.*

29 *Id.*

30 *Id.*

31 "Women in the Workplace," McKinsey & Company & Lean In (2021), p. 7.

32 Angela Morris, "Big Law Onsite Day Care: The Trend That Wasn't," *The American Lawyer* (Jan 13, 2017).

33 "Women in the Workplace," McKinsey & Company & Lean In (2021), p. 49.

34 Gretchen Livingston, "Adult caregiving often seen as very meaningful by those who do it," *Pew Research Center* (Nov. 8, 2018).

35 Gretchen Livingston, "More than one-in-ten U.S. parents are also caring for an adult," *Pew Research Center* (Nov. 29, 2018).

36 *Id.*

37 Alia E. Dastagir, "'Sandwich generation' stress: Adults caring for aging parents face stress, frustration," *Chicago Sun Times via USA Today* (July 13, 2021).

38 Kathleen Kelly, "How to balance your career with the needs of an aging family member," *Pbs.org* (Oct. 23, 2014).

39 "Coping With COVID: The Impact on Sandwich Generation Workers," *The One Brief* (April 7, 2021).

40 Joyce Sterling and Linda Chanow, "IN THEIR OWN WORDS Experienced Women Lawyers Explain Why They Are Leaving Their Law Firms and the Profession," *ABA Commission on Women in the Profession* (2021).

41 *Id.*

42 *Id.*

43 *Id.*

44 *Id.*

45 Emme Hall, "Roadshow Asks: Andrew Comrie-Picard, how did you get to be a world-class stunt driver?" *Roadshow* (July 3, 2017).

46 The full facts of this case are actually gleaned from the appellate decision of the criminal conviction: 287 P.3d 299 (Kan. Ct. App. 20212).

47 Krill, Patrick R. JD, LLM; Johnson, Ryan MA; Albert, Linda MSSW, "The Prevalence of Substance Use and Other Mental Health Concerns Among American Attorneys," *Journal of Addiction Medicine* (January/February 2016 - Volume 10 - Issue 1 - p 46-52).

48 *Id.*

49 *Id.*

50 "THE PATH TO LAWYER WELL-BEING: Practical Recommendations For Positive Change - THE REPORT OF THE NATIONAL TASK FORCE ON LAWYER WELL-BEING," (2017).

51 *Id.*

52 *Id.*

53 *Id.*

54 Esther Perel, "#1 Sign That Relationship Won't Last," (July 22, 2020).

55 Liz Fe Lifestyle Team, "Time To Move On: Moving On From A Past Relationship," *Liz Fe* (Mar 29, 2021).

56 Liz Brown & Amy Impellizzeri, "Op-ed: Expect more lawyers to take their skills elsewhere post-Covid 19," *Boston Business Journal* (July 2020).

57 Iffy Ibekwe, "A Good Night's Rest Is The Answer," *Above the Law* (August 6, 2021).

58 "Action is the Antidote: Finding Happiness with Gretchen Rubin," *Inspiration Loves Company Podcast Episode, with Host Deborah Epstein Henry* #6 (Nov 18, 2020).

59 "THRILLABLE HOURS: ANDREW COMRIE-PICARD, RACE CAR DRIVER," Legal Nomads.

60 Andy Frye, "Lawyer Turned Stunt Driver Andrew Comrie-Picard Talks Rally Racing And Movie Stunts," Forbes (July 18, 2019).

61 Andy Frye, "Lawyer Turned Stunt Driver Andrew Comrie-Picard Talks Rally Racing And Movie Stunts," Forbes (July 18, 2019).

62 "Risa Weaver-Enion: Former Lawyer Turned Wedding Planner," *The Former Lawyer Podcast Hosted by Sarah Cottrell* (Episode 25).

63 "100 Best Jobs," *US News & World Report* (2022).

64 Megan J. Thompson, "Interesting Lawyer Statistics & Facts for 2020-2021," *Legal Reader* (June 30, 2021).

65 "Best Paying Jobs," US News & World Report (2022).

66 Alexis Gracely, "Impact of Student Loan Debt on Young Lawyers," *Inside Higher Ed* (September 23, 2021).

67 "Overcoming the Negative Stigma Associated with Attorneys," Chip LaFleur, *LaFleur.*

68 Niall McCarthy, "America's Most And Least Trusted Professions," *Forbes* (Jan 4, 2018).

69 Jenna Greene, "'Soul suck': Ex-lawyers dish on why they ditched their jobs," *Reuters* (Jan 19, 2022).

70 Shunta Grant, "The Lawyer's Escape Pod Podcast," (Dec 15, 2020).

71 A.J. Serafini, "The Truth Behind the Infamous McDonald's Hot Coffee Case," *The Poole Law Group.*

72 Ben Guarino, "Federal judge: Starbucks is not ripping you off when it puts lots of ice in your iced tea," *The Washington Post* (Aug 25, 2016).

73 Amy Impellizzeri, *Lawyer Interrupted* (ABA Publishing 2015).

74 "Kat Johnston leaves her high intensity in-house attorney job purposefully plan-less," *The Lawyer's Escape Pod Podcast.*

75 *Id.*

76 *Id.*

77 "10 Signs You Should Quit Your Biglaw Job," *The Unbillable Life.*

78 "Darcy Luoma," I KNOW HOW THIS (BOOK) ENDS," Podcast, hosted by Amy Impellizzeri (Aug. 4, 2021).

79 National Task Force on Lawyer Well-Being, "Creating a Movement To Improve Well-Being in the Legal Profession," (August 14, 2017).

80 *Id.*

81 "Using Social Media To Stay Connected," *Health.mil.*

82 "How Veterans Can Navigate Change Through Writing," *Health.mil.*

83 "Translating Military Experience to Civilian Employment," *Health.mil.*

84 Melody Manchi Chao, Sujata Visaria, Anirban Mukhopadhyay, Rajeev Dehejia, "Do rewards reinforce the growth mindset?: Joint effects of the growth mindset and incentive schemes in a field intervention," *Exp Psychol Gen* (2017 Oct;146(10):1402-1419).

85 *Id.*

86 Karen Reivich, Ph.D. and Andrew Shatté, Ph.D, *The Resilience Factor* (Harmony 2013).

87 "3 Lessons from 3 Years of Podcasting," *Lessons of a Quitter Podcast,* Episode 160.

88 National Task Force on Lawyer Well-Being, "Creating a Movement To Improve Well-Being in the Legal Profession," (August 14, 2017).

89 Münch, N., Mahdiani, H., Lieb, K. et al. "Resilience beyond reductionism: ethical and social dimensions of an emerging concept in the neurosciences." *Med Health Care and Philos* 24, 55–63 (2021). https://doi.org/10.1007/s11019-020-09981-0.

90 *Id.*

91 https://www.jessicamedinallc.com/.

92 "How the Sunk Cost Fallacy is Keeping You Stuck," *Lessons from a Quitter Podcast* (October 27, 2020).

93 Bill Perkins, *Die With Zero* (Mariner Books 2020), p. 3.

94 Bill Perkins, *Die With Zero* (Mariner Books 2020), p. 7.

95 *Id.*, at 115.

96 *Id.*, at 122.

97 *Id.*

98 Aliyah Frumin, "How Peloton's Robin Arzón went from corporate lawyer to fitness phenom," *MSNBC* (Aug. 11, 2020).

99 Candice Georgiadis, "Women Of The C-Suite: Julie Schechter and Monika Shah of 'Small Packages' On The Five Things You Need To Succeed As A Senior Executive," *Authority Magazine* (Dec 31, 2020).

100 Any views expressed in this publication are strictly those of the authors and should not be attributed in any way to White & Case LLP.

101 Christine's name has been changed, but not her story.

102 Dana Lynch, "Why I Quit My Law Career to Become an Interior Designer at 45," *Real Simple.*

103 Nadine Waldmann, "Art of the Brick – Nathan Sawaya's Lego Works," *Daily Art Magazine*, (Mar 27, 2019).

104 Kate Whiting, "These are the top 10 job skills of tomorrow – and how long it takes to learn them," *weforum.org* (October 21, 2020).

105 Wendi Weiner, "From Lawyer To Entrepreneur: Tips For Making A Successful Transition Out Of Law," *Above The Law* (April 20, 2021).

106 Thompson v. Monroe College, Docket No. 251896-09 (Bronx County 2009).

107 *Id.*

108 Samantha Stainburn, "Promises, Promises," *The New York Times* (Oct. 26, 2009).

109 Jennifer Shore, "17 LinkedIn Marketing Best Practices," *Smartbug Media* (Jan 16, 2020).

110 *Id.*

111 Brain Dean, "Zoom User Stats: How Many People Use Zoom in 2022?" *Backlinko* (Jan. 06, 2022).

112 *Id.*

113 Jonathan Stempel, "Zoom reaches $85 mln settlement over user privacy, 'Zoombombing,'" Reuters (Aug 2, 2021).

114 Chen Ling, Utkucan Balcı, Jeremy Blackburn, and Gianluca Stringhini, "A First Look at Zoombombing," 2021 IEEE Symposium on Security and Privacy (SP).

115 Suler J. "The online disinhibition effect." *Cyberpsychol Behav.* 2004 Jun;7(3):321-6. doi: 10.1089/1094931041291295. PMID: 15257832.

116 *Id.*

117 Joe Marin, "What Is Clubhouse & Why Is It So Popular?" *Screenrant* (May 30, 2021).

118 Derrick David, "What Happened To Clubhouse?" *Medium* (Aug 26, 2021).

119 *Id.*

120 J Oliver Conroy, "Esther Perel on life after Covid: 'People will want to reconnect with eros'" *The Guardian* (Apr 6, 2021).

121 Esther Perel, *How's Work Podcast*, "Breaking News Has Broken Us," S. 2, Episode 6.

122 *Id.*

123 *Id.*

124 *Id.*

125 *Id.*

126 cems.org.

127 Sherry Turkle, *Reclaiming Conversation* (Penguin 2021), p. 4.

128 Sherry Turkle, *Reclaiming Conversation*, (Penguin 2021), p. 62.

129 Aliyah Frumin, "How Peloton's Robin Arzón went from corporate lawyer to fitness phenom," *MSNBC* (Aug. 11, 2020).

130 *See,e.g.,*Caroline Ceniza-Levine, "Ten People You Need To Have In Your Professional Network," *Forbes* (March 5, 2017).

131 https://www.irelaunch.com/.

132 Jasmine Wright, "Harris talks ambition in women of color after personal attacks during Biden's VP search," *CNN* (Augu 3, 2020).

133 Olivia Harrison, "Why Two Corporate Attorneys Moved Across The Country To Open A Coffee Shop," *Refinery 29* (Nov 30, 2020).

134 "Our Story," Sip & Sonder.

135 Olivia Harrison, "Why Two Corporate Attorneys Moved Across The Country To Open A Coffee Shop," *Refinery 29* (Nov 30, 2020).

136 *Id.*

137 "Our Story," Sip & Sonder.

138 Mike DeSimone and Jeff Jenssen, "From Boardroom To Vineyard: Greg Doody on Leaving Corporate Law for Wine," Forbes (May 14, 2019).

139 https://smallpackages.co/.

140 "Women Who Inspire Us: Julie Schechter Crowdfunded the Capital to Get Her Business off the Ground—All While Working a Full-Time Job," The Every Girl (Jun 14, 2019).

141 https://www.moite.photography/.

142 https://www.clicke.co/post/katrine-moite-attorney-turned-artist.

143 https://www.littlepostagehouse.com.

144 "Life & Work with Loly Orozco," *Voyage LA* (Dec 21, 2020).

145 *Id.*

146 "Lawyer to Baker: How Sarah Truesdell's Business Began to Boom During COVID," *Lessons from a Quitter Podcast*, Episode 121).

147 https://www.sugarbysarahla.com/.

148 Anthony Desiato, Linked In.

149 Documentary filmmaker: https://www.flatsquirrelproductions.com/about/.

150 Kerriann Stout, "An Interview With Lawyer-Turned-Filmmaker Anthony Desiato," (May 11, 2020).

151 https://filmfreeway.com/AnthonyDesiato.

152 Jessica Dubiss, "Haub Law Staff Member and Alumnus Anthony Desiato '12 featured on *Above the Law*," *Pace University* (May 2020).

153 Kerriann Stout, "An Interview With Lawyer-Turned-Filmmaker Anthony Desiato," (May 11, 2020).

154 William Grimes, "Jess Jackson Dies at 81, a Wine Grower With a Taste for Thoroughbred Racing," *The New York Times* (April 21, 2011).

155 City of Houston v. Proler (Tex 2014).

156 City of Houston v. Proler (Tex 2014).

157 https://www.jenerationacademy.com/pages/about-us.

158 https://financialpanther.com/about/.

159 Olga Mack, "Learning To Love Risk, As A Lawyer," *Above the Law* (Dec 9, 2019).

160 https://financialpanther.com/about/.

161 Jenny B. Davis, "These lawyers balance full-time practices with a side hustle that pays," *ABA Journal* (May 1, 2018).

162 Bill Chemero, "Making a Career Change During the Pandemic," *Forbes* (Aug 14, 2020).

163 *Id.*

164 Jenny B. Davis, "These lawyers balance full-time practices with a side hustle that pays," *ABA Journal* (May 1, 2018).

165 Jenny B. Davis, "These lawyers balance full-time practices with a side hustle that pays," *ABA Journal* (May 1, 2018).

166 https://www.rhothomas.com/about/.

167 https://www.rhothomas.com/about/.

168 https://marycobbdesign.com/pages/about.

169 https://artcloud.com/art/eggshell-by-mary-cobb.

170 https://www.centraljerseyfamilylaw.com/our-team/christ.previte/.

171 http://www.lawoffashionblog.com/.

172 Jenny B. Davis, "These lawyers balance full-time practices with side hustle that pays," *ABA Journal* (May 1, 2018).

173 https://www.mockingbirdtravel.com/.

174 "Vanessa Perlman Finds Her Flow Between a Freelance Career and a Travel Business," *The Lawyer's Escape Pod Podcast* (January 26, 2021).

175 *Id.*

176 "Action is the Antidote: Finding Happiness with Gretchen Rubin," *Inspiration Loves Company Podcast Episode, with Host Deborah Epstein Henry #6* (Nov 18, 2020).

177 Daniel Honan, "Neuroplasticity: You can teach an old brain new tricks," *Big Think* (Oct 11, 2012).

178 *Id.*

179 Hertzog C, Kramer AF, Wilson RS, Lindenberger U. "Enrichment Effects on Adult Cognitive Development: Can the Functional Capacity of Older Adults Be Preserved and Enhanced?" *Psychol Sci Public Interest.* 2008 Oct;9(1):1-65. doi: 10.1111/j.1539-6053.2009.01034.x. Epub 2008 Oct 1. PMID: 26162004.

180 Daniel Honan, "Neuroplasticity: You can teach an old brain new tricks," *Big Think* (Oct 11, 2012).

181 "Taxi drivers' brains 'grow' on the job," *BBC News* (Mar 14, 2000).

182 Joseph Pompliano, "The Lawyer Turned 2x Stanley Cup Champion," *Huddle Up* (Jul 8, 2021).

183 Marie Fazio, "Gorilla Glue as Hair Spray? 'Bad, Bad, Bad Idea,'" *The New York Times* (Feb 8, 2021).

184 Victoria Moorwood, "Tessica Brown donates $20,000 of GoFundMe money to reconstructive surgery nonprofit," *Revolt* (Feb 15, 2021).

185 Amisha Yadav, "Coaching Industry: Global Opportunities, Market and Growth," *XMONKS* (Aug 16, 2021).

186 Sai Blackbyrn, "84 Key Life Coaching Statistics For 2022," *Coach Foundation* (January 2022).

187 Tom Fi... Why Professional Coaching Should Expand Beyond Executive... bes (Mar 31, 2021).

188 Sai Bla... rn, "84 Key Life Coaching Statistics For 2022," *Coach Foundation*... nuary 2022).

189 Am... Yadav, "Coaching Industry: Global Opportunities, Market and Growth... *MONKS* (Aug 16, 2021).

190 htt... //coachingfederation.org/ethics; https://www.cce-global.org/credential... g/ ethics/bcc.

191 "C... eer Changers & Lawyers Leaving the Law," Bryce Legal.

192 "Shauna Bryce on Legal Career Transitions," The Lion Group Podcast Episodes (Jan 14, 2020).

193 https://www.headspace.com/about-us.

194 https://www.calm.com

195 Jenev Caddell, "5 Differences Between Coaching and Psychotherapy," *Very Well Mind* (September 17, 2020).

196 *Id.*

197 "Life Coach vs. Therapist: 8 Myths Debunked," *Open Counseling.*

ACKNOWLEDGEMENTS

From Amy:

An enthusiastic and heartfelt debt of gratitude goes out to Nancy Cleary from Wyatt-MacKenzie for supporting our first non-fiction project together. We started this journey before anyone heard of COVID-19, and so the project has changed scope and direction, but your enthusiasm never waivered.

A huge thank you to my co-author, Liz Brown, who has gone from hero, to mentor, to friend in the span of a few short years. I'm so grateful to have you by my side through lots of life's big transitions.

To my colleagues and mentors in the law—from the Court of Federal Claims to Landman, Corsi, Ballaine and Ford to Skadden Arps, there are far too many to name here, but I *will* name the best of the best: Honorable Gary Golkiewicz, Mark Landman, Eleanor Armstrong, Paula Tzivragos, Jerry Cuomo, Tara Roscioli, Shannon Cooper, Chris Cox, Shehzad Hasan. When I look back on my 15 years in the law, the times we spent together are among my favorite memories!

To those that made practicing law—how shall I say this?—more *challenging* than it should have been—colleagues, adversaries, clients —I thank you, too. After all, that which didn't kill me inspired me to write a book (or 2!) about it.

To my family and friends who have never once treated me differently just because I'm a lawyer and always will be. They've loved and respected me anyway, with just the errant lawyer joke delivered over Thanksgiving dinner.

And finally, to my children: Paul, Luke, & Grace. Three years of law school, three passed bar exams, and 15 years of legal training, and I still feel like a novice every time these three geniuses challenge me to a debate. My greatest joy has been watching them start to carve their paths to happiness, on their own terms, with grit and hard work and joy. It feels like maybe they've been paying attention, after all.

From Liz:

My first big thanks go to Amy Impellizzeri, my amazing co-author who inspires me with her brilliance, warmth, energy and style every time we talk. Writing anything is much more fun when you have someone you admire to bounce ideas around with, and there is no better co-conspirator than Amy. I feel lucky to be her friend.

Thank you to every one of the lawyers, former lawyers, and sort-of-lawyers who have shared their stories with me over the years. Whether I learned from them during book club meetings when we barely talked about the books, or over Zoom calls when we were many states apart, or while we were working together in any other capacity, every story has meant a lot to me. Making a meaningful change in your life is hard and heroic, and forging a new path takes up energy that few of us have in abundance. But for anyone who wants to leave the law, having realistic examples to learn from is invaluable. The advice these JDs have given me has helped me learn what successful change looks like. This book is largely an effort to pay forward their generosity.

Huge thanks to my friends and family for their love and support, especially during these past few horrible years. In the depths of losing my parents, and in parenting through a pandemic, and in pivoting on a dime in how we teach our students, their love sustained me. A special thanks to my college classmates who have come together as the most remarkable source of online and IRL support since our 25th reunion. I don't know what I did to deserve you all, but I am eternally grateful to be part of the HR91 family.

Finally, it may not be possible for me to express just how much my husband and daughter's love means to me. Honestly, they put up with so much, and then they bring me dinner. Years ago, my husband barely blinked when I told him that I wanted to leave my partnership and just kind of try things out for a while. Even when we were both out of work for a year, in a major recession, with a newborn, he held steady. When I told him a few years later that I had found my dream job in teaching, which would pay a small fraction of my former salary, he encouraged me to go for it. His unwavering support for whatever I wanted to do, to make my life meaningful, has made everything possible.

If my husband gives me roots, my daughter gives me wings. She inspires me every day with her bravery, her sass, her creativity, her compassion, and her demand for social justice. She brings joy to my life with her drawings, her playlists, and whatever tea she chooses to spill. I delight in seeing how dedicated she is to her friends and to her ideals. She is a passionate advocate for what she believes is right, and a persuasive debater who can turn the tables with the best of them. The opportunities she has to use those gifts are infinite. I can't wait to see what she creates next.

CPSIA information can be obtained
at www.ICGtesting.com
Printed in the USA
BVHW091037300822
645842BV00002B/159